ANDRÉ CHÉNIER

OPERA IN FOUR ACTS

MUSIC BY
UMBERTO GIORDANO

LIBRETTO BY
LUIGI ILLICA

First Produced at La Scala, Milan, March 28th, 1896
First American Production at the Academy of Music, November 13th, 1896

WILDSIDE PRESS

SYNOPSIS

ACT I. opens in the Ball-room at the Chateau de Coigny. Gerard, a servant, is straightening up the room. He is grumbling over his many years of unrequited service. He is secretly in love with Madeleine, the daughter of the Countess. The Countess and Madeleine enter, and discuss the guests who are expected at the ball. The guests arrive, and the Countess receives them graciously. Among the guests are the Abbé, and also André Chénier, a poet. Madeleine makes a wager with her companions that she will make Chénier rhyme, and she approaches him with a request that he favor her with a harmless poem that might amuse a school-girl. He grants her request, and sings to her of the wrongs suffered by the poor, hoping in this way to arouse the seriousness in her. As the dancing is about to begin again, Gerard appears at the head of a group of ragged beggars, who beg for alms. They are driven out by the Countess, and the gayeties are resumed.

ACT II. In Paris, at the Café Hottot, several years later. Chénier meets his friend Roucher at the Café. Chénier has incurred the disfavor of the revolutionists by denouncing Robespierre, and Roucher brings him a passport and urges him to escape, but Chénier refuses. Bersi, Madeleine's old nurse, has brought him an unsigned letter, written by the girl, who begs him to come to her aid. A spy, who has watched Bersi hand the letter to Chénier, reports to Gerard, now one of the leaders among the revolutionists, and tells him where the meeting is to take place. At night-fall, Madeleine comes, and Chénier recognizes her. The spy also recognizes Madeleine, and runs to notify Gerard. Gerard finds them, and the two men fight with swords. Gerard is wounded, and the lovers make their escape.

ACT III. At the Court of the Revolutionary Tribunal. Gerard, now recovered from his wound, enters and makes a plea for money for France, and the people give very generously. The spy comes and informs Gerard of the whereabouts of Chénier, who has been captured, but there is no trace of Madeleine. The spy persuades Gerard to write the indictment against André Chénier, whom he denounces as a dangerous man and a traitor. Madeleine comes to plead for her lover, and is ready to give herself to Gerard in order to save the life of Chénier. Gerard, moved by such love, promises to try to save Chénier. The Judge and Jury enter, and Chénier is brought before them. Chénier defends himself, and Gerard confesses to the court that the indictment had been written by him, and that it was all a lie. The mob, however, demands the life of Chénier, and the Jury comes in with a verdict of "Death".

Act IV. André Chénier is writing verses in the Prison of St. Lazare. Roucher comes in, and they bid each other farewell. Madeleine is also permitted a final interview with Chénier. She bribes the guard to let her take the place of another young woman who is awaiting death, and together Chénier and Madeleine go to the scaffold.

CHARACTERS

André Chénier	Abbé
Madeleine	Mathieu
Bersi	A Spy
Countess	Roucher
Gerard	Fouquier-Tinville
Fléville	Dumas
Major-Domo	Schmidt

Beggars, Fishwives, Sanculots, Gendarmes, Guards, Servants, Etc.

ANDRÉ CHÉNIER.

QUADRO PRIMO.

(*Sala da ballo al Castello di Coigny. All' alzarsi della tela, sotto i comandi di un gallonato* Maestro di Casa, *corrono* Lacchè, Servi, Valletti *carichi di mobili e vasi, completando l'assetto dalla serra.* Carlo Gérard, *in livrea, entra sostenendo con altri servi un pesante sofà.*)

Il Maestro di Casa.

Questo azzurro sofà
là collochiam...

(*Gérard e i lacchè eseguiscono, poi il Maestro di Casa accenna verso le sale interne e vi entra seguito da tutti i lacchè. eccettuato Gérard che, inginocchiato avanti all'azzurro sofà ne liscia le frangie, sprimacciando i cuscini*).

Gérard (*al sofà*).

Compiacente a' colloqui
del cicisbeo
che a dame mature,
porgeva qui la mano!
Qui il Tacco Rosso al Neo
sospirando dicea:
"Oritia... o Clori... o Nice... incipriate,
Vecchiette e imbellettate,
io vi bramo
ed, anzi sol per questo, forse, io v'a-
    mo!"
Tal dei tempi il costume!

(*Dal giardino si avanza il padre di Gérard.—Questi guardando commosso allontanarsi il padre*). . . . . .

Son sessant'anni, o vecchio, che tu ser-
    vi!...
A' tuoi protervi
arroganti signori
hai prodigato fedeltà, sudori,
la forza dei tuoi nervi,
l'anima tua, la mente...
e—quasi non bastasse la tua vita
a renderne infinita
eternamente
l'orrenda sofferenza—
hai data l'esistenza
dei figli tuoi...
Hai figliato dei servi!

(*si asciuga sdegnosamente le lagrime, e torna a guardare fieramente intorno a sè la gran serra.*)

T'odio, casa dorata!
L'imagin sei d'un secolo
incipriato e vano!...
Fasti, splendori, orgogli di Re Sole!
Regno di Cortigiane tu, o Reggenza,
e dei Lebel
onnipotenza
tu, Luigi Lussuria!...
O vaghi dami in seta ed in merletti,
volgono al fin le gaje vostre giornate
e le serate
a inchini e a minuetti!
Fissa è la vostra sorte!
Razza leggiadra e rea,
figlio di servi e servo,
qui—giudice in livrea—
ti grido:—È giunta l'ora della Mor-
    te!—

(*La contessa, Maddalena e Bersi appajono al di là dell'arco d'ingresso alla serra.—La contessa si sofferma a dare alcuni ordini al Maestro di Casa. Maddalena si avanza lentamente con la Bersi.*)

Maddalena.

Il giorno
intorno già s'insera
lentamente!
In queste misteriose
ombre forme fantastiche
assumono le cose!...
Or l'anime s'acquetano
umanamente!...

ANDRÉ CHÉNIER.

ACT I.

(*The Ball-room at the Château de Coigny. As the curtain rises enter the Major-domo, followed by Servants carrying furniture with which to ornament the rooms. Gerard, in livery, helps other servants to carry in a heavy sofa.*)

MAJOR-DOMO.

Set the blue sofa down
There, in its place!

(*The Major-domo moves on to rooms beyond, leaving Gerard behind, who smoothes the cushions of the couch and dusts the faded silk.*)

GERARD (*to the Sofa*).

Thou hast patiently listened,
As gallant beaux to dames whose charms had ripen'd,
Their passion here protested!
Here, Corin came to woo,
As he said with a sigh:
"Orynthia! O Chloris! Oh, nymphs with paint bedizen'd
"To deck your features wizen'd,
"I implore you,
"Have pity upon him who must adore you!"
'Tis the mode of the moment!

(*Gerard's father enters, carrying a flower-stand, and as the old man departs by the garden-way, Gerard gazes at him wistfully.*)

Full sixty years, oh! my father,
Hast thou served them,
Devoting ever to thine arrogant masters
Strength of thy manhood, loyally unbounded;
For them thy limbs have toil'd;
They had thy brain, thy spirit,
And yet, as tho' thy life were not sufficient,
A life of drudgery and toil unending,
Its load of shame and sorrow
By thee hath been transmitted
Unto thy sons! Thou'rt a father to slaves!

(*Surveying the sumptuous apartment.*)

Gilded house, I abhor thee!
Of that vain world the image,
As fair, and false and painted!
Pretty ladies, in rich brocade and laces,
Swift advancing,
Dance minuets and gay gavottes
With your modish airs and graces!
Dance! yet your doom awaits you.
Frivolous, infamous gang!
Lackey, and son of a lackey,
Though a menial, yet your judge, I warn ye:
The hour of doom is nigh!

(*The Countess, Madeleine, and Bersi appear at back. The Countess stops to speak to the Major-domo. Madeleine with Bersi slowly enters.*)

MADELEINE.

The daylight fades;
And dusk around is gently falling:
Now, in the dim mysterious twilight,
Things take another shape,
Ethereal, fantastic;
Now unto weary spirits Nature yields her solace!

GÉRARD (*fra sè*).

Della bellezza
o blanda commozione!
Quanta dolcezza,
per te, nell'anima
soave penetra!
Muojon le idee; tu sopravvivi ai secoli
eterna... e aristocratica,
tu, la Eterna Canzone!
(*entra la Contessa*)

CONTESSA.

Via, v'affrettate
e alla lumiera
luce date!
(*à Gérard*)
E—dite—tutto è pronto?

GÉRARD.

Tutto!

CONTESSA.

I cori?

GÉRARD.

Stanno di già vestendosi.

CONTESSA.

E i suonatori?

GÉRARD.

Accordan gli strumenti

CONTESSA.

A momenti
arriveranno gli ospiti...

MADDALENA.

Uno è il signor?...

CONTESSA.

Uno scrittore emerito...
un romanzier pensionato dal Re,
Anton Pietro Fléville.

MADDALENA.

E l'altro chi è?

CONTESSA.

L'Abate, l'Abatino!...
È un improvvisatore!... Un dicitore!...

MADDALENA.

Un viene dall'Italia?...

CONTESSA.

L'Abate da Parigi! Maddaléna

MADDALENA.

ancor così? Ancor non sei vestita?
(*esce.*)

BERSI (*a Maddalena*).

Sospiri?

MADDALENA.

Sì;—io penso alla tortura
del farsi belle!

BERSI.

Ah tu, sì, belle fai le vesti!—Sì!—
Io le fo brutte—tutte!...
Tutte... Tutte!...

MADDALENA.

Soffoco... moro
tutta chiusa
in busto stretto
sia pur "squame di moro"
o in un corsetto,
sì come si usa,
in seta di nakara!...

BERSI.

Il tuo corsetto
è cosa rara!

MADDALENA.

La orribile gonnella
"coscia-di-ninfa-bianca"
mi inceppa e stanca
mi sfianca tutta
e, aggiungivi un cappello
"Cassa-di-sconto" o quello
alla "Basilio" od alla "Montgolfier."
e tu sei sorda e cieca
e, nata bella,
eccoti fatta brutta.
(*La Contessa rientra.*)

MADDALENA
(*affrontandola corraggiosa*).

Per stasera pazienza!
Mamma, non odi?

CONTESSA.

Sono di già gli ospiti!—

MADDALENA.

Così mi metto:—Bianca vesta
ed una rosa d'ogni mese in testa!
(*esce.*)

GERARD (*aside*).
How from her presence
My soul in sorrow
Doth gladness borrow!
Death, that devoureth all,
Yet over thee hath no might,
Spirit of Beauty divine!

(*Enter Countess.*)

COUNTESS.
Haste now, bestir you!
See that the candles all are lighted!
　　(*to Gerard*).
Then every thing is ready?

GERARD.
Yes, madame.

COUNTESS.
And the singers?

GERARD.
Now for their parts are dressing.

COUNTESS.
And the musicians?

GERARD.
Their instruments are tuning.

COUNTESS.
In a moment
The guests will be arriving.

MADELEINE.
One is . . . Monsieur Fléville.

COUNTESS.
A famous author.

MADELEINE.
And who is the other?

COUNTESS.
The little Abbé.

MADELEINE.
One of them comes from Italy?

COUNTESS.
Yes; Fléville does;
The Abbé comes from Paris.
But what is this Madeleine?
You're not yet dressed, my daughter!
　　　　　　　(*Exit.*)

BERSI (*to Madeleine*).
You're sighing?

MADELEINE.
Yes! to think of all one suffers
For looking beautiful.

BERSI.
But you will make your gowns look far more lovely;
And mine seem always hideous!

MADELEINE.
As in a vice one struggles, gasping,
One's waist encircled in a coat of armour,
That votaries of fashion call a corset.
Oh, villainous invention!

BERSI.
But in your corset you look so charming!

MADELEINE.
When girt in gown appalling,
Closely, so closely fitting
That seams are splitting,
To move is torture!
And then with hat gigantic,
Ultra-romantic,
The very latest style—they call it "Montgolfier"—
Your toilette is completed,
And from a beauty you become a fright!

(*Enter Countess.*)
MADELEINE.
Well, this evening, excuse me!
Mother, do you hear them?

COUNTESS.
Yes, for now the guests have come;

MADELEINE.
I know what I'll wear:
Gown of white; and just a rose in my hair!

　　　　　　　(*Exit*).

(Già si anima tutto il castello.—I valletti corono animatamente in su ed in giù apparecchiando le torcie nell'attesa delle slitte.)

CONTESSA
(nervosa, imparte ordini, ora all'uno, ora all'altro).

Presto avvertite i cori;
ed a tempo opportuno
pastorelle e pastori!
E che non manchi alcuno!
Su; presto, i suonatori in cantoria!
(Il Maestro di Casa annuncia ad alta voce.)

MAESTRO DI CASA.
Madama de Bissy e il cavaliere di Villacerf!...

CONTESSA
(al cavaliere di Villacerf).
Oh! quanto commifò!
Come elegante...
e voi gentil Galante!

MAESTRO DI CASA.
La marchesa d'Entragnes e il barone Berwik!

CONTESSA *(al barone).*
Vera galanteria!

MAESTRO DI CASA.
La duchessa di Villemain e il marchese d'Harcout!

CONTESSA *(al marchese).*
A ben più d'una brama
la vostra dama
accender saprà l'esca!...

MAESTRO DI CASA.
La principessa di Saint-Médard e il conte d'Aubetaire!

CONTESSA *(alla principessa).*
Mi ricordate
i dì della Reggenza...
La Parabère, ecco, mi rassembrate!

MAESTRO DI CASA.
Donna Anna da Torcy e don Enrico de Nangis!

CONTESSA
(a don Enrico de Nangis).
Quanta munificenza!

MAESTRO DI CASA.
La contessa Etiolle d'Etoile e il reverendo Fragmont!

CONTESSA
(alla vecchia dama colla quale senza inchinarsi si abbracciano, vecchia dama che ha a cavaliere un grosso ecclesiastico).
Appariscente e fresca
sempre!—Contessa,
sempre, sempre la stessa!

MAESTRO DI CASA.
La marchesa di Lorge e il conte Fleuri!

CONTESSA
(alla bella marchesina, accarezzandole la guancia).
Come siete vezzosa!
Siete un amore!

MAESTRO DI CASA.
La baronessa Boisguilbert e l'abate Crècy!

CONTESSA *(all'abate Crècy).*
Con voi me ne congratulo...
Quale amica!... Perfetta!...

(alla baronessa).
Sublime! Quanta grazia!
(ad altra dama).
Dotta maestra!... Invero è maestria!
Mirabile toeletta!
(Cavalieri e dame si affannano intorno alla Contessa interrogandola:)
Chi avremo? Dite!
Mesmer?
Dugazon?
L'arlecchino Bordier?...
Vestri?
Jeannot?...

CONTESSA
(misteriosa abbassando la voce).
L'Abate!
    TUTTI *(con gridi di gioja).*
L'Abatino?...
(Entrano Fléville, l'Abate e Chénier.)

MAGGIORDOMO.
Il cavaliere Anton Pietro Fléville.

COUNTESS (*to her servants*).
Hasten to call the singers
And, at the proper time,
The shepherds and the shepherdesses;
See that none be missing;
Hurry! send the musicians up to the stand!

MAJOR-DOMO.
Madame de Bissy and Chev. Villacerf!

COUNTESS.
Oh, How stylish
And fashionable you are!
A gallant cavalier indeed!
    (*to Villacerf*).

MAJOR-DOMO.
The Marquise d'Entragnes and Baron Berwick!

COUNTESS.
Vastly gallant, I vow! (*to the Baron*).

MAJOR-DOMO.
The Duchess of Villemain and the Marquis of Harcourt!

COUNTESS.
Oh! take care, my lord Marquis!
Your lady's eyes will surely work fresh havoc! (*to the Marquis*).

MAJOR-DOMO.
The Princess of St. Médard and the Count of Aubetaire!

COUNTESS.
You remind me
Of the days under the Regency
And of the beautiful Parabére!
    (*to the Princess*).

MAJOR-DOMO.
Donna Anna da Torcy and Don Henry de Nangis!

COUNTESS.
What a kingly guest! (*to Nangis*).

MAJOR-DOMO.
The Countess d'Etoile and Rev. Fragnont!

COUNTESS.
Why, you're as fair and young as ever!
Yes, Countess, just as youthful as ever! (*to the old dame*).

MAJOR-DOMO.
The Marquise of Sorge and Count Fleury!

COUNTESS.
Oh! How sweet and charming;
How lovely you are!
    (*to the Marquise*).

MAJOR-DOMO.
The Baroness Boisguilbert and the Abbé Crécy!

COUNTESS.
I congratulate you;
Your friend is perfectly sweet!
    (*to the Abbé*).
Sublime! How graceful!
    (*to the Baroness*).
Very clever indeed!
You're wonderfully dressed!
    (*to another lady*).
(*The hostess is being surrounded by inquisitive guests eagerly questioning her:*)
Do tell us who is coming!
Will he be Mesmer?
    Or Dugazon?
That harlequin Bordier?
  Is he Vestri?
    Or Jeannot?

COUNTESS.
(*mysteriously, in a whisper*).
The Abbé!

ALL (*joyously*).
The little Abbé!

MAJOR-DOMO.
Chevalier Antoine Pierre Fléville.
(*Enter Fléville, the Abbé, and Chénier.*)

FLÉVILLE.
Commosso... lusingato...
a.. tanti complimenti
e... a questo, più che omaggio...
...amabil persiflaggio!...
Ch'io vi presenti Flandro Fiorinelli,
è cavaliere, italiano e musico!
e Andrea Chénier...
un che fa versi e... che promette molto.
 (*Maddalena entra*).

IL MAGGIORDOMO (*annuncia*).
Sua Reverenza l'Abate...
(*Le dame a questo annuncio si commuovono, rompono l'ordine fino allora tenuto e rumorosamente, con piccoli gemiti di gioja, attorniano il*

MARITI.
Ha ceduto?

L'ABATINO.
Fu male consigliato!...

CONTESSA.
Necker?

L'ABATINO.
Non ne parliamo!
(*Degusta la marmellata sospirando in atto di suprema afflizione.*)

TUTTI.
Quel Necker!...

DAME

I CAVALIERI.
Dite?

I MARITI.
Che novelle della Corte?

LE DAME.
Noi siam curiose!

I CAVALIERI.
Presto!

TUTTI.
Dite! dite!

L'ABATINO.
Debole è il Re...

di Enrico IV!

TUTTI.
Orrore!

DONNE.
Dove andremo a finire?...

L'ABATINO.
Cosi giudico anch'io!

CONTESSA.
Non temono più Dio!

L'ABATINO.
Assai, madame belle,
sono dolente de le mie novelle...

ANDRÉ CHÉNIER

FLÉVILLE.
Delighted, I assure you,
At this auspicious meeting;
And flattered, vastly flattered,
By such a cordial greeting!
Let me present Fernando Fiorinelli,
A distinguished Italian musician—
André Chénier—writer of verses,
Who so they say, has talent!

(*Enter Madeleine*).

MAJOR-DOMO.
His reverence the Abbé!
(*The Ladies leaving their places in confusion rush toward the new comer and eagerly surround him. The Abbe is fairly smothered with courtesies.*)

THE LADIES.
The Abbé at last!
It is the Abbé.

THE GENTLEMEN.
At last!

MADELEINE.
So you've just come back from Paris!

CHORUS.
From Paris?

THE LADIES.
Is it true?

THE GENTLEMEN.
Anything new?

COUNTESS.
What news at Court, I pray you?

MADELEINE.
We are dying to hear,

THE LADIES.
Yes, do tell us, please!

CHORUS.
Let us hear, quickly!

ABBÉ.
The King, alas, is weak!

THE GENTLEMEN.
Is he yielding?

ABBÉ.
He has been ill-advised!

COUNTESS.
Ah, Necker!

ABBÉ.
(*Sadly helping himself to a marmelade.*)
Let us not speak of him!

CHORUS.
That Necker!
We are dying to know; yes, we are!

ABBÉ.
(*Vigorously attacking the marmelade with his spoon.*)
We've now the "Third Estate"!

CHORUS.
Oh! Oh! This seems absurd!

ABBÉ.
And they've insulted even—

CHORUS.
Whom?

ABBÉ.
The statue of Henri Quatre!

CHORUS.
Oh, horror!

THE LADIES.
Gracious! where will it end?

ABBÉ.
That's what I'd like to know!

COUNTESS.
No fear have they of God!

ABBÉ.
Enough, my beauteous ladies;
Much am I griev'd no gladder news to bring you!

FLÉVILLE.
Passiam la sera
allegramente!—Della primavera
a i zefiri gentili
codeste nubi svaniranno! Il sole
noi rivedremo e rose e gigli e viole
e udrem ne l'aria satura de'fiori
l'eco ridir l'egloghe de' pastori—

TUTTI (*a vicenda*).
O soave bisbiglio!
È il vento!
È zefiro!...
È mormorìo di fonte!...
È fruscìo d'ali
Bacio è di nubi!...
Molce il cuor!
Vallea
veggiamo aprica!
Io, un prato!
Un ruscelletto
ascolto mormorar!
Parlan le fronde!
Sospira un salce!
Querula la canna
di Dafne geme.
Ecco il suo gregge!
Rezzo
divin!

FLÉVILLE.
È questo il mio romanzo!

PASTORELLI.
Pastorelli, addio! Ne andiamo
verso, ahi! lidi ignoti e strani!
Ahi! sarem lungi dimani!
Questi lochi abbandoniamo!
Non avrà, fino al ritorno,
gioje il cuore!
Non piacer fino a quel giorno,
non amore!

PASTORELLI.
O pastori, ahi! che dolori
agli acerbi vostri detti!
Treman dentro ai nostri petti
languidetti i nostri cori!
Ed... ahi! ahi! fino al ritorno
che crucîori!
Non piacer fino a quel giorno,
non amori!

L'ABATINO.
"Il Volpe e l'Uva, favola.
"Un volpe rodomonte—sospinto dalla
    fame
"sovra alta vite tremula, vermilia
"rama carca di grappoli
"adocchia e cura
"ammaliato.
"Ma... oh!... come
"tropp' alto pende il pampino!
"E il volpe esclama: Oh, cosa vana
"l'uva immatura!—
"E, sospirando, s'allontana!
"Del volpe chi sa il nome?...
"Terzo stato!"

CONTESSA (*si avvicina a Chénier.*)
Signor Chénier...

CHÉNIER.
Madama la Contessa?

CONTESSA.
La vostra Musa tace?

CHÉNIER.
È una ritrosa
che di tacer desìa.

CONTESSA.
La vostra Musa è la Malinconia!
        (*à Fléville*).
Davver poco cortese!

FLÉVILLE.
È un po' bizzarro!

ABATINO.
Musa ognor pronta è donna a molti
    vieta!...

CONTESSA.
Musa ognor pronta!... È ver... Ecco il
    poeta!...
(*Prende il braccio dell'Abatino e con
lui si avvicina a Fiorinelli, inducendolo gentilmente al clavicembalo*).

MADDALENA (*alle compagne*).
Io lo farò poetare! Scommettiamo?...
        (*si avvicina a Chénier*).

MADDALENA.
Al mio dire perdono ed al mio ardire!..
Ma viva bramosìa.
mi spinge... Poi... son donna e son cu-
    riosa!
Bramo di udire...
un'egloga da voi o una poesia
per monaca o per sposa.

LE AMICHE.
Benissimo!
Per monaca o per sposa!

FLÉVILLE.
What matters that, my friends?
We'll all be merry;
And ere returns the spring-tide,
With light, and scent of flowers,
Dispers'd shall be the storm that lowers!
There, on a bank of violets and fragrant roses,
The breeze shall bear to us, on pinion light,
Echoes of song, chants of the merry shepherd!
'Tis the sigh of the breezes!

ABBÉ.
'Tis the zephyrs!

CHORUS.
'Tis the wind!

FLÉVILLE.
'Tis the murmor of the fountain!

CHORUS.
'Tis the sound of wings!

ABBÉ.
Methought I heard the rippling stream!

FLÉVILLE.
Behold, my dream comes true!

CHORUS.
Oh, gentle nymphs, adieu!
To lands afar we're flying.
Oh, hear us, a-sighing!
Heigho! Heigho!
To distant lands we roam
Before the morrow;
To part with you, alas!
Brings bitter sorrow.
Ah, well-a-day!
Adieu! we must away!

CHORUS.
Alas! The bitter pain
In our trembling heart
Now that we must part
Heigho! Heigho!
Until you come back
How it will ache
And our mind will rove
For want of pleasure
And of love!

ABBÉ.
A hungry fox was spying
With an envious eye
The sweet ripe grape
Hanging from a high vine
But seeing that it was
So hard to reach it
She went away musing:
It is sour after all!
Now that fox has a name
And it is?—"Third Estate."

COUNTESS (*approaching Chénier*).
Monsieur Chénier!

CHÉNIER.
Madame, your most obedient!

COUNTESS.
Your Muse, in truth, is silent!

CHÉNIER.
Aye, for 'tis wayward,
And rather would be dumb!

COUNTESS.
Your Muse is Melancholy so it seems!

(*to Fléville*).
Indeed, 'twas scarcely courteous!

FLÉVILLE.
He's so eccentric!

ABBÉ.
Rare is the dower of ready song, we know it!

COUNTESS.
Well said! Behold our poet!
(*Takes the Abbé's arm and approaches Fiorinelli, whom she leads to the harpsichord*).

MADELEINE (*to her companions.*)
I'll make him rhyme, I warrant!
Shall we wager?
(*approaches Chénier*).

MADELEINE.
I would pray you to pardon
My seeming boldness;
A woman, as you know,
Is nothing, if not curious.
Will you not favour us with something of your own?
Some harmless poem—that might amuse a school-girl?

CHORUS.
That might amuse a school-girl!

CHÉNIER.
Desio che muove da due labbra rosa
è comando gentile a gentil cuore.
Ma—ohimè—la fantasia
non si piega a comando o a prece umile...
è capricciosa assai la poesia...
a guisa dell'amore!...
  (Maddalena e le ragazze ridono.)

CONTESSA.
Perchè ridete voi?
Che c'è?
Che c'è?...
Che avviene?
Dite!

LE AMICHE.
Udite! Udite che il racconto è bello!
Il poetino è caduto in un tranello.

MADDALENA.
A tua preghiera, mamma, disdegnoso
opponeva un rifiuto...
Allor bizzarro
pensier mi venne...

LE AMICHE.
È vero...
La vendetta!

MADDALENA.
Io dissi: Scommettiano?...

CONTESSA E TUTTI.
Di che cosa?

MADDALENA.
Che nel risponder alle preci nostre
volgarmente parlato avria d'amore.

CONTESSA.
Ebben?

TUTTI.
Ebben?

CHÉNIER (in atto di preghiera).
No, signorina!

MADDALENA.
Ebbene...
          (imita Chénier).
Levò la fronte al cielo!—
Chiamò la Musa!—E la implorata musa
per sua bocca ridisse la parola
che a me voi,
          (si rivolge ad un vecchio ridicolo).
voi,
          (a un abate).
e voi,
          (a un marchese grasso).
e voi, più volte
(a un giovinotto strano per la sua bruttezza).
a me dite ogni sera... senza Musa.
          (tutti ridono).

CHÉNIER.
5 Colpito qui m'avete... ov'io geloso
celo il più puro palpitar dell'anima.
Or vedrete, fanciulla, qual poema
è la parola "Amore" per voi scherno!
6 Un dì all'azzurro spazio
guardai profondo,
e ai prati colmi di viole,
pioveva l'oro il sole
e folgorava d'oro
il mondo;
parea la Terra un immane tesoro,
e a lei servìa di scrigno il firmamento.
Dal cuore de la Terra a la mia fronte
veniva una carezza viva, un bacio.
Gridai, vinto d'amore: T'amo, t'amo
tu che mi baci, tu divinamente
bella, o patria!
E volli pien d'amore
pregar!...
Varcai d'una chiesa la soglia;
là un prete ne le nicchie
de'santi e de la Vergine
accumulava doni... e al sordo orecchio
un tremulo vegliardo invano
chiedeva pane e invan stendea la mano!
          (Sensazione).
Entrai nell'abituro;
un uom vi calunniava bestemmiando
il suolo che l'erario a pena sazia
e contra a Dio scagliava e contro a li uomini
le lacrime de' figli.
In cotanta miseria
e di cose e di genti—qui la patrizia prole
a che pensa e che fa?
Sol l'occhio vostro esprime umanamente
qui un guardo di pietà,
ond'io ho guardato a voi sì come a un angelo.
E dissi: Se bugiardo fu il miraggio
che mi venne dal sole,
eccola la bellezza della vita
nel glauco raggio
soave di pietà che vibra in voi!

CHÉNIER.
Your request, mademoiselle,
Is for me a command.
Yet, alas! sweet Fancy's coy,
Nor will heed, though commanded,
Or e'en entreated.
A most capricious is the Muse,
As fanciful as Love!

(*Madeleine and her friends burst out laughing*).

COUNTESS.
What causes all this mirth?

CHORUS.
What is it?
Oh, listen, for 'tis vastly diverting!
He is trapped in a way most disconcerting.

MADELEINE.
When your entreaty, mother,
He curtly refused,
I thought I'd try—'twas in sport—

CHORUS.
Just for mischief!

MADELEINE.
I said: Girls, let us wager—

COUNTESS.
Wager what, pray?

MADELEINE.
That I would make him speak of love!

COUNTESS.
Yes—well?

MADELEINE (*mockingly*).
The Muse he summoned;
And she, the nymph capricious,
Thro' his lips hath discoursed
Of the theme of which to me—
(*addressing a ridiculous dotard*).
You!
(*to an Abbé*).
And you!
(*to a fat Marquis*).
Ah, yes, and you, too,—
(*to a singularly ugly youth*),
And you, often speak,
Unaided by the Muses!

(*General mirth*)

CHÉNIER.
Your scorn hath touched me here,
Where jealously are guarded
All the secrets of the soul inviolate:
You shall know, now, fair maiden,
What a poem lies in that little word "love,"
By you thus derided!
I gaz'd o'er the blue expanse of heav'n unclouded;
O'er fields with violets enamell'd;
The world around, above me,
In glimm'ring golden glory was shrouded;
The spacious earth seem'd as one mighty gem
Enclosed within her casket, the boundless heaven!
Softly from earth, to me as a greeting,
There floated upon the wanton breezes a caress!
Then, in a transport I cried:
Ah! I love thee, my country,
Divine in all thy beauty, oh land, mine own!
By Love inspired, I sought to pray;
Swift thro' a church-door then I pass'd:
A priest collected offerings for the Virgin,
By all the faithful given; yet never heeded
Nor heard its piteous pleading
Of one poor aged beggar,
With hands held out in vain!

(*Sensation*).

And then a workman's hut I enter'd,
Where one in desperation loudly curs'd his country;
He curs'd his rich employers;
To God above in fury,
And unto men he hurl'd them,
His children's bitter tears!
Ah! ye pamper'd patricians,
How do ye right all this wrong?
'Twas in your eyes alone,
Oh, lovely maiden, that gentle pity seem'd to dwell,
And so I turn'd to you, as to an angel fair, and said:
"Love from out those beauteous eyes is shining!"
But when, as in scorn you addressed me,
'Twas then that my heart by grief anew was shaken!

Ma, poi,
a le vostre parole,
un novello dolore
m'ha còlto in pieno petto...
O giovinetta bella, d'un poeta
non disprezzate il detto:
Udite!—Amate pria
e prima di schernir sappiate Amore!

(*Indignazione generale*).

MADDALENA (*a Chénier*).
Perdonatemi!

CONTESSA.
Creatura strana assai! Va perdonata!..
È capricciosa e un po' romantichetta.
Ma... udite!... È il gajo suon de la gavotta.
Su, cavalieri!—Ognun scelga la dama!...

(*Mentre i servi fanno posto e i cavalieri e le dame si preparano, lontanissime, si sentono venire avvicinandosi confuse cantilene.*)

LE VOCI (*si avvicinano.—Sono lugubremente dolorose, gemiti che risuonano cupi e minacciosi*).
La notte e il giorno
portiamo intorno
il dolore;—
Siam genti grame
che di fame
or si muore;—
A mammelle avvizzite
chieggon le vite
de' bimbi moribondi!
Affamati, languenti
cadiam morenti
sovra suoli infecondi!

(*All'arco d'ingresso della serra appare Gérard alla testa di una folla di gente stracciata*).

GÉRARD (*imitando il maggiordomo*).
È Sua Grandezza la Miseria!

(*mentre quegli straccioni, lamentosamente stendendo le mani, susurrano:*)

Anime umane,
deh, le nostre preghiere
non ci tornino vane!
Genti cristiane,
sollievo a queste fiere
torture aspre, inumane!

CONTESSA (*livida dall'ira*).
Chi ha introdotto costoro?
GÉRARD.
Io, Gérard!

CONTESSA (*ai suoi valletti, lacchè*).
Questa ciurmaglia via!
(*a Gérard*).
E tu pel primo!

GÉRARD.
Sì, me ne vo—Contessa!
questa livrea—m'è di tortura;
è vile per me il pane
che qui mi sfama!
La voce di chi soffre a sè mi chiama!
Vien, padre mio, con me!
(*al padre che intercede*).
Perchè ti curvi ai piè
di chi non ode voce di pietà?
(*poi, strappandosi la livrea di dosso, grida:*)
Dalle mie carni via questa viltà

CONTESSA (*imbizzita*).
Via!... Via!... Via!..

(*Il Maestro di Casa, i servi, i lacchè, gli staffieri, respingono la folla.—La Contessa si lascia cadere sul sofà ansante dalla bile*).

CONTESSA.
Ah! quel Gérard!... L'ha rovinato il leggere!...
Credetemi... Fu l'Enciclopedia!...
Ed io... che... tutti i giorni... facevo l'elemosina
e... a non fare... arrossire... di sè la povertà...
perfin m'ho fatto... un abito costume di pietà!...
(*al Maestro di Casa che torna*).
Son tutti andati?

MAESTRO DI CASA.
Sì.

CONTESSA (*agli invitati*).
Scusate! L'interrotta,
mie dame, ripigliamo, gentil, nobil gavotta
Invitate le dame!
Ritorni l'allegria!

CALA LA TELA.

Believe me, beauteous maiden—
The word of a poet, oh, despise not!—
Oh, hearken! Naught do you know of love!
Hear me—Love is divine;
Spare it your scorn!
The flame that lights the universe,
'Tis Love!
(*General indignation.*)

MADELEINE (*to Chénier*).
Pray you, pardon me!

COUNTESS (*to her Guests*)
She's such a flighty girl!
(*to Madeleine*).
There, I forgive you!
She's so capricious!
Inclin'd to be romantic!
But listen! The merry sound of the gavotte!
Now, cavaliers, pray choose your partners!

(*As the dance is about to begin, a dismal sound of chanting is heard without. Gerard appears at the head of a group of ragged beggars.*)

CHORUS OF PAUPERS.
Each day, each morrow,
Brings woe and sorrow;
For bread we're crying;
Our children are dying.
We're starving! Will none hear us calling?
Oh, save us from famine appalling!

GERARD (*mimicking the pompous Major-domo*).
His Serene Highness, Prince Poverty!

COUNTESS (*angrily*).
Who admitted those beggars?

GÉRARD.
'Twas I, Gerard!

COUNTESS.
Out! drive the rabble out!
And go you first!

GERARD.
Yes, I'll be gone, my lady!
I'll doff this hateful livery
That I loath and detest!
Your bread, your food, it chokes me,
While round me all my fellow-men are starving!
(*to his father, who intercedes*).
Come, father, come with me!
Why dost thou bend the knee to them,
Since pity dwells not in their hearts!
(*stripping off his livery*).
Off with this livery vile!
Off, badge accursed!

(*The footmen eject the beggars and Gerard is hustled out.*)

COUNTESS (*as she sinks prostrate upon a couch*).
Oh! that Gerard!
'Tis reading that has ruined him!
To me, of all people!
I who daily give away unto the poor!
Through regard for their feelings,
When I supply their needs,
I wear a modest gown, designed
For charitable deeds!
(*to the Major-domo.*)
They have all gone, then?

MAJOR-DOMO.
Yes, my lady!

COUNTESS (*to her guests*).
Excuse me, ladies fair!
Our gavotte, by your leave, let us finish.
Now mirth once more shall reign!

CURTAIN.

QUADRO SECONDO.

(Parigi in un giorno del Giugno 1794, col Caffé Hottot e la Loggia dei Fogliantisti. A dritta un altare dedicato a Marat con su un busto di questi. Dietro la, "Cours-la-Reine" e il ponte Perronet sulla Senna. Chénier seduto solo ad una tavola. Mathieu "Populus" indica ad Orazio Coclite il busto di Marat che egli ha tolto dall'altare e ripulisce, a sferzate energiche di fazzoletto, dalla polvere).

MATHIEU.
Per l'ex inferno!
ecco ancor della polvere
sul capo di Marat!...
(strizza l'occhio all'amico e accenna alla Bersi seduta con la Spia.)
Che ci covasse scherno?...
Ah, troppo spesso
da un poco sgualdrineggiano
quelle donnine là!...
È male!... male!... male!...
Benedetto, o Rasojo nazionale!...
Tu sol, tu solo non risenti il sesso!...
(Entrano degli strilloni. Mathieu compra un giornale, ma si accorge che é vecchio.)
M'ha appioppato un giornale
di cinque mesi fa!

BERSI *(all'Incredibile.)*
È ver che Robespierre allevi spie?...

L'INCREDIBILE.
Vuoi dire, cittadina "Osservatori dello spirito pubblico..."

BERSI.
Come tu vuoi.

L'INCREDIBILE.
Non so,
nè lo posso sapere!
Hai tu a temere?

BERSI.
Temer?... Perchè? Perchè temer dovrò?
Non sono, come te, una vera figlia
autentica della Rivoluzione?
Amo viver così!... Vivere in fretta
di questa febbre gaja d'un godere
rapido, acuto e quasi inconsciente!...
Qui il giuoco ed il piacere... là la morte!...
Qui il suon de le monete e il biribisso!
Laggiù il cannone e il rullo de'tamburi!
Qui inebria il vino... laggiù inebria il sangue
Qui riso e amore;
là si pensa e s'odia!
Qui la Meravigliosa e l'Incredibile
che brindan col Bordeaux, collo Sciampagna;
(Verso l'ex Cours-la-Reine di dove sbocca il "piccolo paniere" carico di condannati condotti alla ghigliottina.)
le mercatine là e le pescivendole
e la carretta di Sanson che passa!
(esce.)

L'INCREDIBILE.
No, non m'inganno! Era proprio con lei
la bella bionda!... Ho scovato la traccia!...
(estrae di tasca un piccolo taccuino e vi scrive su rapidamente:)
La cittadina Bersi, far sospetto
di corruzione non spontanea;
guardò Chénier di sottecchi. Osservarla!
Andrea Chénier per qualche ora in attesa
con febbril ansia evidente. Osservarlo!
(esce.)
(Roucher entra dal Cours-la-Reine.)

CHÉNIER *(vedendolo).*
Roucher!

ROUCHER.
Chénier!... Tutto il giorno ti cerco!
La tua salvezza tengo!...

CHÉNIER.
Un passaporto?

ROUCHER.
Qui tutto intorno è periglio per te!
La tua preziosa vita salva—parti!

CHÉNIER.
Il mio nome mentir!.. Fuggire!... No!.

ACT II.

(The Scene shows us Paris on a day in June, 1794, with the Café Hottot and the Terrasse des Feuillants. To the right an altar dedicated to Marat, on which stands his bust. At the back, the "Cours la Reine" and the Peronnet Bridge across the Seine. At one of the tables Chénier is seated alone. Mathieu and Horace are arranging the altar, and Mathieu is dusting Marat's bust with a handkerchief. Bersi and the Spy are seen at one of the tables.)

MATHIEU.
By all that's infernal! There's still such a heap of dust on the head of Marat!

(Newsboys enter and Mathieu buys a paper. Soon he discovers that it is an old one.)

Why, he's sold me a paper that's fully five months old!

BERSI *(to the Spy)*.
Is it true that Robespierre has chartered spies?

SPY.
Not "spies," my worthy citizen;
"Observers of the temper of the public!"

BERSI.
As you will!

SPY.
I know not;
Indeed, why do you ask me?
Are you afraid, then?

BERSI.
Afraid? Not I!
What cause have I to fear?
Am I not, like yourself, a true and loyal child
Of the glorious Revolution?
No life but this for me!

Swift as a whirlwind, borne ever onward
Down the tide of pleasure;
Never a pause to think;
Not a moment of leisure;
Here, gambling, song, and laughter;
And yonder, death!
Here, chink of golden louis and rattle of dice-box;
There, boom of cannon, rolling of the drum!
Here, wine intoxicates;
Down there, they're drunk with blood!
Here, smiles and friendship; there, undying hate!
While here we quaff our brimming bumper of champagne,
Out in the market, there,
Folk sell their fish and fruit—
Meanwhile the headsman's cart goes past!

(The death-cart passes, followed by an excited crowd.)

(Exit.)

SPY *(aside)*.
I'm not mistaken!
'Twas with her I saw the blonde-hair'd beauty!
Now the clue I've discovered!

(writing in his book.)

"Citoyenne Bersi rouses suspicion
Of conduct one may call seditious.
She gave Chénier such a sly glance!
Watch her closely!
André Chénier here several hours has waited,
No doubt for some important message.
Watch him closely!"

(Exit).

(Roucher enters from the Cours la Reine.)

CHÉNIER *(seeing Roucher)*.
Roucher!

ROUCHER.
Chénier!
All day long have I sought you!
Here I have it! your safeguard!

CHÉNIER.
Ah! 'Tis a passport!

ROUCHER.
On ev'ry side there is danger for you;
Ah! Save your life; 'tis precious; flee!

CHÉNIER.
What? Escape like a coward?
Not I!

ROUCHER.
Te ne prego, Chénier!

CHÉNIER.
Credi al destino?...
Io credo!... Credo a una possanza arcana
che benigna o maligna i nostri passi
or guida or svia pei diversi sentieri
de l' esistenza umana!—Una possanza
che dice a un uomo:—Tu sarai poeta!
A un altro:—A te una spada, sii soldato!
Or bene, il mio destin forse qui vuolmi!...
Se quel che bramo mi si avvera, resto!

ROUCHER.
Se non si avvera?...

CHÉNIER.
Allora partirò!
Seguo il destino umano dell' amore.
Io non ho amato ancor!...
Pure sovente—nella vita
ho sentita
sul mio cammin vicina
passar la donna che il destin fa mia;
passare tutta bella—ideal, divina
come la poesia;
passar con lei sul mio cammin l'amor!
Si più volte ha parlato
la sua voce al mio cuore;
udita io l'ho sovente
con la sua voce ardente
dirmi: "Credi all'amore;
tu sei Chénier, amato!
(*e preso sottobraccio Roucher lo allontana dal caffè Hottot, narrandogli confidenzialmente.*)
Da tempo mi pervengon strane lettere
or soavi ed or gravi—or rampogne, or consigli!
Scrive una donna misteriosa ognora!
In quelle sue parole vibra un'anima!
Chi sia, indagato ho invano!

ROUCHER.
Ancor?...

CHÉNIER.
Finora!
Ma or guarda!

ROUCHER (*legge*).
Qui un ritrovo?

CHÉNIER.
Ah! la vedrò!

ROUCHER.
La misteriosa alfin solleva il velo!...

CHÉNIER.
Non ridere!

ROUCHER.
Vediam!
Calligrafia
invero femminil! Carta elegante!...
Ma, ohimè! profumo "alla Rivoluzione!!"
Questo gentil biglietto,
a profumo di rosa,
provocatore,
non m'inganno, io giuro,
esce da un salottino
troppo noto all'amore:
Chénier, te l'assicuro,
il tuo destino
ti ha dato il cuor... d'una Mergvigliosa
Riprendi il passaporto e... via la lettera.

CHÉNIER.
Non credo!

ROUCHER.
Tu non credi?

CHÉNIER.
No, non credo!

ROUCHER.
La femminil marea parigina
in gaje onde irrequiete or qui rovescia!
Io le conosco tutte! Passeranno,
ed io ti mostrerò la misteriosa!

CHÉNIER (*colpito*).
Una Meravigliosa
la bella creatura
del mio pensier sognata?!
Non donna, ma...

ROUCHER.
Nay, hear me, Chénier!

CHÉNIER.
No! No!
Do you believe in Fate, as I do?
Faith have I in a secret power
That guides the steps of mortals,
For good, or else for ill,
Along the devious pathways of existence.
'Tis this that says to one man: "Be a poet!"
And to another: "Wield the soldier's sword!"
Maybe Fate bids me to stay here!
If what I long for come to pass, I'll stay.

ROUCHER.
If not, what then?

CHÉNIER.
Why, then, my friend, I'll go!
The destiny that guides me
No other is than Love.
I never yet have loved!
Though the bright presence long-desir'd
Of beauteous lady hath my life inspir'd;
Of one alone
That fate shall make mine own!
Ideal divine; star of my stormy sea;
With her, then life were Paradise for me!
Full oft in my dreams,
Like some strange melody haunting,
Her voice from out the midnight
Calls me in tones enchanting,
And murmurs: "Love is divine!"
"Chénier, at last 'tis thine! 'tis thine!"
For long while past, strange letters I've received;
Sometimes charming,
Or alarming,
To reprove me or to warn me!
It is a woman writes
In such strange fashion;
Her words upon the page
They glow with passion;
Vainly I sought to find her.

ROUCHER.
Vainly, did you say?

CHÉNIER.
Until now,
But see here!

ROUCHER.
A rendezvous?

CHÉNIER.
At last I shall meet her!

ROUCHER.
The mysterious woman unveils!

CHÉNIER.
Why do you laugh?

ROUCHER.
Let me see!
ROUCHER (*looking at letter*).
Aye, 'tis indeed a thorough woman's hand!
Choicest of paper!
But oh! the perfume reeks of Revolution!

This little dainty letter,
With its perfume designed the senses to fetter,
Chénier, I swear it, believe me,
It comes from a *salon* noted
For the cult of the tender passion.
The Fate you trust rewards you with the heart
Of some fine dame of fashion!
Come! take your passport; fling aside the letter!

CHÉNIER.
I doubt you!

ROUCHER.
Do you?

CHÉNIER.
Rather!

ROUCHER.
The modish dames of Paris
By way of diversion, frequent this café;
I know them all by sight; and as they pass
To you will I point out your most mysterious fair!

CHÉNIER (*in amazement*).
Some fine lady of fashion,
She, the beautiful being divine
Of whom I dreamed?
Not a woman, but—

ROUCHER.
...una cosa.

CHÉNIER.
Una caricatura?!
Una moda?!

ROUCHER.
..Una faccia imbellettata!

CHÉNIER.
La sconosciuta mia?

ROUCHER.
La tua divina
soave poesia

CHÉNIER.
in fisciù a la Bastiglia!...
...ed il nero alle ciglia?!

ROUCHER.
...e con rimesse chiome!...

CHÉNIER.
Oh, cosa senza nome!...
Accetto il passaporto!...

ROUCHER.
É provvido consiglio!

ROUCHER.
Vedi? al ponte Peronnet
s'agglomera la folla.

CHÉNIER.
La eterna cortigiana!
Vi si schiera
per incurvar la fronte
al nuovo iddio!

MATHIEU.
Evviva Robespierre!

CHÉNIER (accennando a Robespierre).
Egli cammina solo.

ROUCHER.
E quanto spazio ad arte fra il nume e
i sacerdoti! Ecco Tallien!...

CHÉNIER.
L'enigma!

ROUCHER.
Ultimo, vedi?

CHÉNIER (ironico).
Robespierre il piccolo!

LA FOLLA.
Ecco laggiù Gérard!
Gérard!... Viva Gérard!

(Entra Gérard.)

LA FOLLLA (entra Robespierre).
Evviva Robespierre!
Barère!
  Collot d'Herbois!
Quello è Couthon!
   Saint-Just!
    David.
Tallien!
 Fréron!
  Barras!
    Fouché!
Le Bas
 Sieyès!
Thuriot!
 Carnot!
  e Robespierre!

L'INCREDIBLE (a Gérard).
La donna che mi hai chiesto di cercare
è bianca e bionda?...

GÉRARD.
Azzurro occhio di cielo
sotta una fronte candida;
bionda la chioma con riflessi d'oro
una dolcezza in viso
ed un sorriso
di donna non umano;
nel suo vestir modesto;
pudico velo
sovra il tesoro
d'un puro sen virgineo
ed una bianca cuffia sulla testa.
—Dammi codesta creatura vaga!
ti dissi—Cerca! Indaga!
Dinanzi mi è passata qual baleno
un di, ma poscia
io l'ho perduta!
Io piu non vivo; peno!
Mi salva tu da questa grande angoscia
e...tutto avrai!...

L'INCREDIBILE.
Stasera la vedrai!

ROUCHER (a Chénier).
Eccole!.. Strani tempi! Là vanno
 i pensatori.
Qui lo stormo chiassoso, di que' vivi
 bagliori.
Tu presso a me ti poni! Di qui facile
 cosa
sarà scoprir chi sia la tua misteriosa!

ROUCHER.
A mere thing.

CHÉNIER.
Just a caricature or a fashion plate?

ROUCHER.
A painted face.

CHÉNIER.
That of my unknown Dame?

ROUCHER.
The beauteous lady that your life inspired
Wears a Bastille foulard.

CHÉNIER.
And has darkened lashes?

ROUCHER.
And hair all crimpled.

CHÉNIER.
Oh! the nameless thing!
Here! Give me the passport!

ROUCHER.
Aye, take my good advice!
See how yonder, by the bridge,
A surging mob assembles.

CHÉNIER.
The eternal courtesan
Bending low, in abject adoration
To their new idol.

MATHIEU.
Long live Robespierre!

CHÉNIER (*pointing to Robespierre*).
He goes alone.

ROUCHER.
And what gulf 'twixt idol and adorers!
Here comes Gallien....

CHÉNIER.
The sphynx.

ROUCHER.
And Robespierre's brother
Comes last.

CHÉNIER (*ironical*).
A little Robespierre.

(*Enter Gerard.*)

THE MOB.
There goes Gerard! Long live Gerard!
(*Enter Robespierre.*)
Long live Robespierre!
Barère!
Collot d'Herbois!
Here is Couthon!
   Saint-Just!
      David!
Tallien!
   Fréron!
      Barrar!
         Fouché!
Les Bas,
   Sieyès!
      Thuriot!
         Carnot!
            Robespierre!

SPY.
The lady whom you bade me seek, pray, tell me,
Is she pale and fair?

GERARD.
Her eyes are blue as the heavens;
Whiter than snow her beauteous brow
And all her hair more bright than burnish'd gold;
The sweetest of all faces;
Her smile hath graces
Entrancing to behold;
Most neat her dress and simple;
She wears a wimple,
White, yet not whiter than her bosom sweet;
It shrouds her head, and at her waist doth meet.
Find me this lovely maid that I adore;
I pray you search, explore!
Before my gaze she flashed
Like a flame in the night;
But now that I have lost her,
Life is void of delight!
If from this torture you can save me,
Then all is yours!

SPY.
This evening you shall see her!

ROUCHER.
Here they come! Strange times, indeed!
First march the careworn thinkers,
Then the seekers of pleasure!
And now, as they pass by us,
We'll mark your dame mysterious.

CHÉNIER.
Partiamo!

ROUCHER.
Guarda! Guarda!

CHÉNIER.
No! non voglio: partiamo!

BERSI (*a Roucher*).
Non mi saluti?

(*Rapidamente gli susurra.*)
Qui trattien Chénier.
Son spiata! qui fra poco tornerò!

L'INCREDIBILE.
Procace Bersi,
qui sono ancor per te! Meco giù scendi?

BERSI (*sorridendogli indifferente*).
Per poco?

L'INCREDIBILE.
Non ti chiedo che una Trenitz.

BERSI.
E perchè no?

L'INCREDIBILE.
Scendiam?

BERSI.
Scendiam!
(*Scendono nei sotterranei del Caffè.*)

LE MERAVIGLIOSE (*vedendo Barras discendere nei sotterranei del Caffè Hottot.*)
Ah, riderem davver.
E là Barras!
La sua rivoluzion nome ha "piacer"
Ci aspetta là
fra il giuoco ed il bicchier.
Siam Riso, siamo Baci, siamo Amor
anche in di di Terror.
Uno oggidi baciato diman muor...
Vedove... e spose ognor.
Repubblicani, eroi o aristocratici
che importa a noi,
purché sia Amor?
Amante innamorato
cosi lo vuole il cuor
soltanto e ognor!...
Siam Riso, siamo Baci, siam l'Amor..
Vedove... e spose ognor!...

(*Scendono nei sotterranei del Caffè.*)

CHÉNIER.
Una meravigliosa!

ROUCHER.
Ho indovinato?
Son male esche d'abbocco!...

CHÉNIER.
Tuttavia...
Che mi vuol dir?...

ROUCHER.
É sera!... Ora propizia!
E all'alba di domani... Via!... In cammino!

CHÉNIER.
O mio bel sogno, addio!...
(*Si vede ritornare la Bersi.*)

BERSI.
Andrea Chénier!
Fra poco, a te, una donna minacciata
da gran periglio qui verrà.
Là attendi!

CHÉNIER.
Dimmi il suo nome!...

BERSI.
Il suo nome... Speranza!

ROUCHER.
La ignota tua scrittrice! No... è un tranello!

CHÉNIER.
Io là verrò!...
(*Bersi fugge via*).

ROUCHER.
É un agguato.

CHÉNIER.
M'armerò!...

ROUCHER.
Ah! veglierò su lui! (*Escono*).
(*E già sera.*)
(*Mathieu riappare. Viene a dar lume alla lanternina dell' altare a Marat.*)

L'INCREDIBILE (*esce guardingo dal Caffè e va a porsi allo sbocco della via laterale al caffè, nascondendovisi dietro l'angolo.*)
Ed il mio piano è fatto!... Ora attendiamo!

(*Una forma di donna si avanza cautamente*).

CHÉNIER.
Let us depart.

ROUCHER.
Now just look there!

CHÉNIER.
No. Let's go.

BERSI (*to Roucher*).
Won't you salute me?
(*In a rapid whisper.*)
Beware! Keep Chénier here!
I'm being watched!

SPY.
My good friend, Bersi,
I'm at your service, now;
Shall we go in, then?

BERSI.
If you like.

SPY.
I should like some light refreshment.

BERSI.
So should I! Let's go!
(*They enter the café.*)

CHORUS.
Ah! We will make merry
With that Barras
Whose revolution is "pleasure."
He's down here
Gambling and drinking.
Even in these days of terror
We like to laugh, to kiss and to love.
The man you kiss to-day will be dead
    by to-morrow,
And we are in turn widows and brides.
Republicans, heroes or aristocrats,
What do we care
As long as they love us?
A fervent lover,
That's what our hearts crave for.
We like to laugh, to kiss and to love,
And to be in turn widows and brides.
(*They enter the café.*)

CHÉNIER.
A lady of fashion!

ROUCHER.
I guessed as much!

CHÉNIER.
What could she tell me?

ROUCHER.
'Tis night-fall! hour most propitious;
Before the morrow dawns, escape! Begone!

CHÉNIER.
Ah! lovely dream, farewell!
(*Bersi hurries out of the café and approaches Chénier.*)

BERSI.
André Chénier!
Ere long to you a lady
Threaten'd by grievous peril
Will come; await her here!

CHÉNIER.
Tell me her name!

BERSI.
Her name is "Speranza."
                (*Exit.*)

CHÉNIER.
Now we shall meet.

ROUCHER.
Your unknown correspondent.
Nay, 'tis a trap, an ambush!

CHÉNIER.
I'll get my sword!

ROUCHER.
Ah! I'll protect him, now!
             (*Exeunt.*)
(*It is now growing dark. The patrol passes, and Mathieu enters with a lantern, which he places on the altar. The Spy enters, on the watch for Madeleine.*)

SPY.
So! All my plans are laid!
Here I'll await them! (*Hides.*)

MADDALENA.
Viene l'altare...
(*si guarda intorno; è impaurita di quel silenzio*).
Nessuno!... Ho paura!

L'INCREDIBLE.
Ecco già il maschio!
(*entra Chénier*).

MADDALENA.
Ah, è lui!
Andrea Chénier!

CHÉNIER.
Son io!...
(*Maddalena tenta parlare, la commozione sua è grande e non può profferire parola.*)

CHÉNIER.
(*sorpreso di quel silenzio.*)
Deggio seguirti?...
(*Maddalena risponde con un gesto: No!*)
Sei mandata?...
Dimmi da chi? Di' chi mi brama!

MADDALENA.
Io, sono!

CHÉNIER.
(*sorpreso ed ingannato all'abbigliamento da officiosa di lei*).
Tu? Ebben, che sei?—Di!

MADDALENA.
Ancor ricordi?... Ascolta!...
(*e Maddalena, per richiamarglisi alla mente, gli ricorda le parole che Chénier le ha rivolto la sera del loro incontro al castello di Cogny.*)

CHÉNIER.
Sì: mi ricordo!... Udita io ti ho di già!...
Ah nuova la tua voce non mi parla.
Ch'io ti vegga!...

MADDALENA.
Guardatemi!

CHÉNIER.
Ah, Maddalena di Coigny!...

L'INCREDIBLE.
Ah è lei! La bionda!... Or tosto da Gérard!
(*e cautamente si allontana*).

CHÉNIER.
Voi? Voi!...

MADDALENA (*atterrita*).
Guardate là!

CHÉNIER.
Dove?

MADDALENA.
Là!.. Un'ombra!

CHÉNIER.
(*va all'angolo dove prima era l'incredibile, ma non vede alcuno*).
Nessun!... Pur questo loco è periglioso
E qui... sola...

MADDALENA.
Fu Bersi che l'ha scelto.
Or essa è là, giù, al giuoco e se un periglio...
ne minacciasse... Sono un'officiosa
che le viene a recar la sua mantiglia!

CHÉNIER.
La mia scrittrice?... Voi la mia celata
amica ognor fuggente?!

MADDALENA.
Eravate possente;
io invece minacciata;—
pur nella mia tristezza
pensai sovente d'impetrar da voi
pace e salvezza,
ma... non l'osai!
E ognora il mio destino
sul mio cammino
vi sospingea!
Ognora io vi seguivo, e strano assai,
ognor pensavo a voi
come a un fratello!—
E allora vi scriveva
quanto il cuore o il cervello
dettavami alla mente.
Sì, il cuore mi diceva che difeso
avreste quella che v'ha un giorno offeso.
Al mondo Bersi sola mi vuol bene
(è lei che m'ha nascosta). Ma da un mese
v'ha chi mi spia e m'insegue. E Bersi pure!
Mutammo nascondiglio, e più veemente
era la caccia!... Ove fuggir?... Fu allora
che pure voi non più potente seppi,
e son venuta.—Udite! Sono sola!
Son sola e minacciata! Io più non reggo!
Son sola al mondo! Sola ed ho paura
Io spero in voi! Proteggermi volete?

MADELEINE (*enters cautiously*).

Here is the altar!
As yet there's no one. How I tremble!

(*Enter Chénier.*)

'Tis he!
André Chénier!

CHÉNIER.

'Tis I! Say, shall I follow?
Who sent you thither? Who needs my help?

MADELEINE.

I do.

CHÉNIER.

And who are you?

MADELEINE.

Do you remember?

CHÉNIER.

Yes—I remember!

MADELEINE (*repeating his words addressed to her once at Coigny*).

"Naught do you know of Love!
"Hear me—Love is divine;
"Spare it your scorn!"

CHÉNIER.

Where have I heard that strange, sweet voice?
Let me see you!

MADELEINE.

Behold my face!

CHÉNIER.

Ah! Madeleine de Coigny! You!

SPY (*aside*).

'Tis she! the blonde!
Now I'll inform Gerard!

(*Exit.*)

MADELEINE (*terror-struck*).

See yonder there! A phantom!

CHÉNIER.

There's no one!
And yet this place is one of peril!

MADELEINE.

'Twas Bersi chose it;
But if danger now should threaten
I'll play the serving-maid
Who's brought a mantle for her mistress.

CHÉNIER.

You, my fair scribe?
Was it you the friend so long unknown,
And lost so long?

MADELEINE.

In the day of your power
By peril grave was I threaten'd;
Yet often in my sadness
I fondly hop'd to gain thro' you
Safety and gladness.
I dar'd not, then; but now 'tis Fate's decree
That thrown together we should be.
Hope had I no other;
My trust I gave to you—
Gave, as to a brother.
Then, letters oft I wrote you,
By heart or brain dictated,
In days and hours ill-fated.
I knew your loyal heart
Would have nobly requited
Her who long since your genius slighted.
In all the world no friend have I but Bersi;
('Twas she who help'd to hide me!)
But now for a month by spies am I hunted;
How to escape?
Then came the news that you had fall'n from pow'r;
To you I come!
Ah! hear me! I'm alone, beset by danger;
All helpers fail me,
Dark fears assail me,
Oh! say, will you protect me?
In you I trust!

CHÉNIER.
Ora dolcissima,
sublime ora d'amore!...
Possente l'anima
sfida il terrore!...
Tu mi fai puro il cuore
d'ogni viltà!...
Bramo la vita,
ma non temo la morte.
Ora dolcissima
che segni la mia sorte,
deh, rimani infinita!

MADDALENA.
Vicina nei perigli?—Vicina nel terrore?...

CHÉNIER.
Sì! Vieni al braccio mio! Tu sei l'amore!...
Fino alla morte insieme?

MADDALENA.
Fino alla morte insieme!
(*Appena Chénier e Maddalena hanno fatto pochi passi, dietro il Caffè corre verso di loro Gérard, seguito dall'Incredibile.*)

GÉRARD.
Maddalena, contessa di Coigny!

MADDALENA (*terrorizzata*).
Gérard!

GÉRARD.
A guisa di notturna
io vi ritrovo a notte intorno...

CHÉNIER.
Segui
per la tua strada e non dar noja a gente
che si rincasa!...

GÉRARD.
(*avventandosi contro Chénier per strappargli Maddalena.*)
È merce proïbita!

CHÉNIER (*a Roucher*).
Salvala!

GÉRARD (*all'Incredibile*).
Fugge!... Inseguila!

ROUCHER.
(*spiana contro all'Incredibile un pajo di pistole da tasca*).
A te bada!...

L'INCREDIBILE.
(*arretra e appigliandosi a più prudente consiglio*).
Alla sezione!
(*e fugge*)

GÉRARD.
(*buttandosi armato di spada contro a Chénier*).

CHÉNIER.
Ah, tu non sei che un frate!... Sei Chabot?...
Io ti rubo a Sanson!

GÉRARD (*ferito, cadendo*).
Son còlto!...

CHÉNIER.
L'hai voluto!...

GÉRARD.
Odi, Chénier...
Fuggi!... Il tuo nome già Fouquier Tinville
ha noto!... Va...
Proteggi Maddalena!
(*Chénier fugge.*)
(*Entra Mathieu—L'Incredibile con guardie nazionali.*)

MATHIEU.
Gérard ferito?!

L'INCREDIBLE
Il feritore...

LE MERAVIGLIOSE.
Assassinato? Chi?

GÉRARD.
(*sollevandosi, fa uno sforzo e guardando l'Incredibile trova ancora l'energia di impedirgli di parlare, balbettando:*)
Ignoto!...
(*e sviene*)

MATHIEU.
L' han fatto assassinare i Girondini!

ALCUNI.
Gérard!

LE MERAVIGLIOSE.
Gérard?

Morte agli ultimi Girondini!

CALA LA TELA.

CHÉNIER.

Hail! bright golden hour,
For which my heart was yearning!
By Love's immortal pow'r
My grief to gladness turning!
Thou of earthly baseness
Shalt purify this heart!
Tho' life's joys invite me,
Death shall ne'er affright me!
Golden hour of love, ah! stay!

MADELEINE.

In danger's hour beside me,
To guard me and to guide me!

CHÉNIER.

'Tis Love's bright star shall guide us;
Pale Death may ne'er divide us.

MADELEINE.

In life, in death, forever thine!
(*As they are going, enter Gerard, who bars their passage.*)

GERARD.

Madeleine de Coigny!

MADELEINE (*horror-struck*).

Gerard!

GERARD.

At night-fall, here I find you? And disguis'd?

CHÉNIER.

Stand back, sir! Go your ways!

GERARD.

GERARD (*endeavoring to seize Madeleine.*)
Forbidden fruit!

(*Roucher and the Spy enter.*)

CHÉNIER (*to Roucher*).

Save her!

GERARD (*to the Spy*).

Follow her!

ROUCHER (*threatening the Spy*).

Back there! (*Exit with Madeleine.*)

SPY.

I'll fetch the gendarmes!
(*Exit.*)
(*Gerard draws his sword and attacks Chénier.*)

CHÉNIER (*mockingly*).

Why, you fence like a friar or a clown!

GERARD (*furiously*).

I'll rob the headsman of his prize!

CHÉNIER.

Are you not Chabot?

GERARD.

I am wounded.

CHÉNIER.

It's your own fault.
(*Gerard is wounded, and falls.*)

GERARD.

Ah!
You are Chénier! Then flee!
Your name's on Fouquier-Tinville's death-list!
Begone! Save Madeleine!
(*Chenier escapes.*)

(*Enter Mathieu, the Spy, and others, with gendarmes.*)

MATHIEU.

Gerard is wounded.

SPY.

And his assassin—is—

CHORUS.

And his assassin?—

GERARD (*with a desperate effort to prevent the Spy from speaking.*)
I know not! (*Swoons.*)

MATHIEU.

The Girondins have done this bloody deed!

THE MEN.

Gerard!

THE WOMEN.

Gerard!

CHORUS.

Death to the villains, one and all!

CURTAIN.

QUADRO TERZO.

(*L'aula del Tribunale rivoluzionario. Accanto a un' urna colossale su'l banco della presidenza Mathieu arringa la folla e sollecita contribuzioni*).

MATHIEU.

...Dumouriez traditore (muoja presto!)
è passato ai nemici (il furfantaccio!);—
Coburgo, Brunswick (Pitt crepi di peste!)
e il vecchio lupanare dell'Europa
tutta, contro ci stanno!... Oro e soldati!
Onde quest' urna ed io che parlo a voi
rappresentiam l'imagin della patria!

(*Un gran silenzio accoglie il discorso di Mathieu, però nessuno va ad offrire*).

Nessun si muove? Che la ghigliottina
ripassi a ognun la testa e la coscienza!

(*Alcuni, pochi, vanno e gittano nella grande urna oggetti e denari. Mathieu riprende*).

È la patria in periglio!... A Nostra Donna
il vessil nero sventola! Io pure
or, come già Barère, io levo il grido
di Louverture: Liberta' e patate!

(*vedendo sopraggiungere Gérard*).

Ma, to'... laggiù à Gérard! Convalescente
appena accorre ove il dover lo chiama.
Ei vi trarrà di tasca gli ex luigi
con paroline ch'io non so...
M'infischio
io de' bei motti... Ed anche me ne vanto!

TUTTI.

Cittadino Gérard, salute!...
Evviva!

MATHIEU.

La tua ferita?

GÉRARD.

Grazie, cittadini!
La forte fibra mia m'ha conservato
alla mia patria ancora!

MATHIEU (*indicandogli l'urna*).

Ecco il tuo posto!

(*poscia sempre colla sua voce monotona accennando al drappo si rivolge al pubblico ripetendo*).

È la patria in pe...

(*ma, accortosi che la pipa gli si è spenta, conclude indicando Gérard*).

Cedo la parola.

GÉRARD (*con vero accento di dolore*).

Lacrime e sangue dà la Francia!
Udite!
Laudun ha inalberato
vessillo bianco!
È in fiamme la Vandea!
E la Bretagna ognora ne minaccia!
E Austriaci, e Prussiani, e Inglesi, e tutti
nel petto della Francia
gli artigli armati affondano!
Occorre e l'oro, il sangue!
L'inutil oro e gemma ai vostri vezzi,
donne francesi, date!
Donate i vostri figli alla gran madre,
o voi, madri francesi!

LE DONNE.

(*commosse, gittano dentro tutto quanto hanno in dosso di denaro o d'ornamento*).

Prendi!... È un ricordo!
A te! Un anello!
È un braccialetto!
Otto dì di lavoro!
Una fibbia d'argento!
Quanto posseggo!
Son due bottoni d'oro!

(*S'avanza una vecchia cieca con un giovinetto quindicenne*).

LA VECCHIA.

Fatemi largo, fatemi!
Son la vecchia Madelon; mio figlio è morto;
avea nome Roger; morì alla presa
della Bastiglia; il primo figlio suo
ebbe a Valmy galloni e sepoltura.
Ancora pochi giorni, e io pur morrò.
È il figlio di Roger! L'ultimo figlio,
l'ultima goccia del mio vecchio sangue...
Prendetelo!
Non dite che è un fanciullo!
È forte!... Può combattere e morire!...

ACT III.

(*The Court of the Revolutionary Tribunal. On the President's table a colossal urn, near which stands Mathieu, haranguing the crowd, and inviting contributions.*)

MATHIEU.

Dumouriez the traitor, the villain,
Has gone over to th' enemy! (lying scoundrel!)
Coburg and Brunswick,
(Pitt, the devil take him!)
That ancient lupanar call'd Europe,
All are in arms against us!
Money and soldiers! That's what we need.
This urn and I we're pleading now to-day
For funds to help our country!

(*Profound silence; yet no one contributes.*)

Will none come forward?
Then may the guillotine make short work of you all!

(*Some advance and throw contributions into the urn.*)

Our country's in danger!
Barére, he's told you so,
And to my cry now listen all:
"What's a home without ha'pence?"
(*As Gerard approaches.*)
But here's our worthy Gerard!
Maybe he'll draw the money from your pockets
With words that I could never find.
A plague on pretty speeches!
They're not my style at all!

CHORUS.

To our worthy Gerard welcome and greeting!

MATHIEU.

Your wound is better?

GERARD.

Thank you, fellow-citizens: my constitution's sound;
'Tis this hath sav'd me yet to serve my country.

MATHIEU (*to Gerard*).

Your place is there!

(*Drawling out once more:*)
And the country's in—

(*Finding that his pipe is out and stopping short.*)
(*to Gerard.*)

Speak to them yourself!

GERARD.

Citizens!
France now sheds her tears of blood!
Loudun the white flag has hoisted;
La Vendée is in flames; Brittany threatens us;
While Austria, Prussia, England—all Europe
With vast and mighty armies
Now strives to crush our Fatherland!
She needs your gold, your blood!
The useless gold on all your trinkets,
Women of France, now give!
And give your stalwart sons to the Great Mother,
Mothers of France!

(*The women fling coin and trinkets into the urn.*)

THE WOMEN.

Take them! They're my ear-rings!
And this! Here's my bracelet!
My brooch! And here's my last week's wages!
Here's an old silver buckle!
And here are two gold buttons!
Here's all I possess!
Here's my little cross!

(*And old blind woman advances with a lad of fifteen.*)

OLD WOMAN.

Make way, there!
I am old Madelon!
My son is dead; his name was Roger:
He was killed at the siege of the Bastille.
His eldest boy, who fought at Valmy,
Promotion won, yet perish'd.
'Tis but a little while and I shall die!
Here I've brought you Roger's son,
The youngest, the last;
He's all I live for; he is all I love!
Take him! Don't say he's but a child!
He's strong, though, and for France can fight and die!

GÉRARD.
Noi l'accettiamo! Dinne il nome suo?

LA VECCHIA.
Roger Alberto.

GÉRARD.
A sera partirà!
(*allora la vecchia abbraccia forte il fanciullo che la bacia*).

LA VECCHIA.
Prendetemelo via!

LA VECCHIA.
Chi mi dà il braccio?...
(*Brancola intorno per un appoggio e vien condotta fuori*).

CORO
(*ballando al suono della Carmagnola*)
Amici, orsù! Beviam! Danziam ognor
Colmo bicchier—Allieta il cor!
Cantare e ber!
Viva la libertà!
Danziam la Carmagnola
al tuon, al suon—del cannon!

(*L'Incredibile si avvicina a Gérard*).

L'INCREDIBILE.
L'uccello è nella rete!

GÉRARD.
Lei?!...

L'INCREDIBILE.
No; il maschio.
È al Lussemburgo!

GÉRARD.
Quando?

L'INCREDIBILE.
Stamattina.

GÉRARD.
E come?

L'INCREDIBILE.
Il caso!

GÉRARD.
Dove?

L'INCREDIBILE.
Là a Passy,
presso a un amico.

GÉRARD.
E lei?

L'INCREDIBILE.
Nessuna traccia!
Ma tal richiamo è il maschio per la femmina
che volontariamente (penso e credo!)
essa a noi ne verrà.

GÉRARD.
No; non verrà!...
(*Lontano un gridìo acuto e confuso da ogni parte.*)

L'INCREDIBILE.
Ascolta!

GÉRARD.
Grida son...
Monelli aizzati.

L'INCREDIBILE.
No; i soliti strilloni!
(*Passa—e lo si vede dall'arco di ingresso della sezione—venendo dalla via di destra—une strillone che urla a tutta gola:*)
L'arresto importantissimo
d'Andrea Chénier, nemico della patria!

L'INCREDIBILE.
Queste grida
arriveranno a lei!

GÉRARD.
Va, tentatore!
E poscia?... Ebben?

L'INCREDIBILE.
Donnina innamorata
che d'aspettar s'annoja,
se è già passata
l'ora e il perchè non sa
di quel ritardo del suo amico al nido,
sfido! (e ch' io muoja!)
se la bella presaga
all'ansia vinta
non ti discende ratta per la via
così, com'è, discinta!
Esce correndo... E indaga!
E vola! E scruta! E spia!
To'! passa uno strillone? E vocia un nome?
Oh, come tutta impàllida!
Ma non vacilla o china!..
Possanza dell' amor!
In quel dolor
cessa la donna ed eccola eroina!
Tutto oserà!
Laonde, per mia scienza
tu la vedrai! Pazienza!
Sì, a te verrà!
Sì; questo è il mio pensiero
un po'incredibll, ma altrettanto vero!

GERARD.
Yes, we'll accept him. What is his name?

OLD WOMAN.
Albert Roger!

GERARD.
He'll be sent away to-night.

OLD WOMAN (*as she tearfully bids the lad good-bye.*)
Darling, good-bye!
Take my darling boy!
Who will give me an arm?

(*Groping for support, she is led out.*)

CHORUS (*as they dance to the tune of the Carmagnole*).
Come dance and drink, good friends, to-day;
With song and wine drive care away!
The flagon fill that cheers the heart,
And bids all sorrow swift depart.
Drink, then, to Freedom's cause!
Down with the despot's laws!
We'll dance the Carmagnole,
Though loud the cannon roar!

SPY (*approaching Gerard*).
The bird is in the snare!

GERARD.
She?

SPY.
No, the man!
He's at the Luxembourg.

GERARD.
Since when?

SPY.
Since this morning.

GERARD.
Why, how's that?

SPY.
A mere chance!

GERARD.
Where was he?

SPY.
At Passy, at his friend's.

GERARD.
And she?

SPY.
As yet, no trace of her;
But for the "she" the "he" has such attraction,
That, if I'm not mistaken,
She'll come back of her own accord.

GERARD.
Nay, she'll not come!
(*Cries heard without.*)

SPY.
Do you hear the street-lads selling papers?
(*Boy passes shouting out, "Arrest of André Chénier!"*)
That cry is bound to reach her ears!

GERARD.
What of that?

SPY.
When love-sick dame, complaining,
Awaits her laggard lover,
And trysting-time is over,
What resource has she remaining?
Alarm'd and most dejected
To find herself neglected,
If love won't bind him,
She'll go herself and try to find him!
Swift thro' the streets she's flying,
And watching, waiting, prying—
Ha! There's a newsboy bawling;
What's that he's calling?
What name? Oh, Heaven, his name!
Endow'd with courage stoic,
By Love's tremendous pow'r,
In grief's dark hour,
Weak woman gains a fortitude heroic!
For Love she would risk all!
Mark what I say; 'tis true.
Patience! She'll come to you
Before the fall of night.
It sounds unlikely; but I'm right!

GÉRARD.

Ah, ancor più fieramente m'odierà!

L'INCREDIBILE.

Che importa? Nella femmina
vi sono assai distini corpo e cuore!
Tu scegli il corpo!—È la parte migliore.
Stendi l'atto d'accusa!—Andrea Chénier
Sia tosto al Tribunal, qui, deferito!
Fouquier Tinville aspetta.

GÉRARD.

Ah, se avvenisse...

L'INCREDIBILE.

Scrivi!...

GÉRARD.

Ed essa...

L'INCREDIBILE.

Scrivi!...

GÉRARD.

Esito dunque?—Andrea Chénier segnato
ha già Fouquier Tinville!—Il fato suo
é fisso!—Oggi o diman...
(deponendo la penna)
No, è vile! È vile!

L'INCREDIBILE.

Oh, come vola il tempo!... Affollan già le vie...

GÉRARD.

(riprende la penna; riflette).
Nemico della patria?!
(ride)
È veccia fiaba!...
(scrive)
Beatamente ognor la beve il popolo.
(scrive)
Nato a Constantinopoli?...
(riflette, poi esclama e scrive:)
Straniero!
Studiò a Saint-Cyr?...
Soldato!...
Di Dumouriez un complice?
Traditore!
È poeta?
Sovvertitor di cuori e di costumi!...
Poi... m' ha ferito?... Scrivo "odio politico!"

(ma a quest' ultima accusa la penna
gli fugge dalle mani)

Un di m' era di gioja passar fra morte e morte
fra gli odi e le vendette, puro, innocente e forte!
Dà sangue or fango e lacrime la mia superba idea..
Un vil piccino io sono!...
Gigante mi credea!...
Io sono sempre un servo!...
Ho mutato padrone!...
Sono il servo obbediente di violenta passione!
Ah, peggio!... Uccido e tremo!
Così fra sangue e fango
senza coraggio passo, e, mentre uccido, io piango!
Io della Redentrice figlio pel primo ho udito
il grido suo pel mondo e vi ho il mio grido unito...
Or smarrita ho la fede nel sognato destino?...
Com' era irradiato di gloria il mio cammino!...
La coscienza nei cuori ridestar de le genti!...
Raccogliere le lacrime dei vinti e sofferenti!...
Vincere le tenèbre!... Diritto la Sapienza!...
Dovere l'Eguaglianza!... L'amore Intelligenza!...
Fare del mondo un Pantheon!... Gli uomini in dii mutare
e in un sol bacio e abbraccio tutte le genti amare!...
Ah, di Chénier la voce fu, voce d' poeta
che luminosa allora tracciata m'ha la meta.
Or rinnego il poeta?—Rinnego il santo grido
che m' ha redento?—Ah in lui la mia coscienza uccido!
Sol l'odio!... L'odio!... L'odio!... Io d'odio ho colmo il cuore
e chi così mi ha reso, fiera ironia! è l'amore!
Sono un voluttuoso!... Ecco il novo padrone:
il Senso!... — Bugìa tutto! Sol vero la Passione!

L'INCREDIBILE.

Sta bene! — Ove trovarti se...

GÉRARD.

Qui resto!
(L'Incredibile si allontana.)

GERARD.

The fiercer, then, her hate for me!

SPY.

What matter?
There are two parts to a woman—
Her body and her soul.
You choose her body: of the two, 'tis the better!
Now, draw up the indictment!
André Chénier must be denounced to the Tribunal!
Fouquier-Tinville awaits him! Write!

GERARD.

But should it happen....

SPY.

Write!

GERARD.

That she....

SPY.

Do write, I say!

GERARD (*aside*).

Why do I hesitate?
André Chénier marked out by the Attorney-General?
Ah! then his fate is seal'd to-day or to-morrow.

(*Throws down the pen.*)

No! 'tis vile!

SPY.

Haste! for the time is flying.
And all the streets are throng'd.

GERARD (*musingly*).

The "Enemy of his Country"?

(*Laughing.*)

Ah! that's an old tale;
But one that never fails to touch the mob.

(*Writing.*)

"Born at Constantinople; an alien;
"Student at St. Cyr; a soldier;
"and a traitor; Dumouriez's accomplice; a poet; a dangerous man; a sower of sedition."

(*The pen falls from his hand.*)

Time was when I rejoic'd
That passions vile could never sway me;
Innocent, pure, and brave,
I deem'd myself a giant;
I'm still a slave!
'Tis a mere change of masters!
I'm now but the bondsman of infamous passion!
Worse than that! A murderer sentimental,
Who while he murders, weeps!
Son of the glorious Revolution,
When first her cry "Be free!" rang thro' the world,
To her voice my own then made reply:
How have I fallen from my glorious pathway!
Once, like a line of radiant light it lay before me!
To establish the hearts of all my fellow-comrades;
To bid the mourner weep no more,
Console the weary suff'rer,
Make of this world a Paradise,
Where men should be as gods, divine;
To bind all comrades in one vast embrace!
The holy task I now abandon.
With hate my heart is fill'd!
What wrought this change? Irony grim! 'Twas Love!
I'm a mere voluptuary;
The master I serve now is Passion!
All else is false! The one thing real is Passion!

SPY (*reading the indictment*).

'Tis well! Where shall I find you, if—

GERARD.

I shall be here!

(*Exit Spy.*)

MADDALENA (*entrando*).

Carlo Gérard?

MATHIEU.

Sì; c'è! — Entra! — Sta là!

MADDALENA (*con voce tremante*).

Se ancor vi sovvenite
di me, non so!
Son Maddalena di Coigny.
Ah, non m'allontanate!... Deh, mi udite!

GÉRARD.

Io t'aspettava! Io ti voleva qui!...
Io son che come veltri ho a te lanciato
orde di spie!
Entro a tutte le vie
la mia pupilla è penetrata
e ad ogni istante!
Io, per averti qui, preso ho il tuo amante!

MADDALENA.

A voi! — Qui sto!
Signore, vendicatevi!

GÉRARD.

Non odio!

MADDALENA.

Vendicatevi! Son l'ultima
del nome mio!

GÉRARD.

Non odio!

MADDALENA.

Perchè, dunque, m'avete qui voluta?

GÉRARD.

Perchè ciò è scritto nella vita mia!
Perchè ciò è scritto nella vita tua!
Perchè ciò volle il mio voler possente!
Era fatale, e, vedi, s'è avverato!...
Io l'ho voluto allora
che tu piccina
giù pel gran prato
con me correvi lieta in quell'aroma
d'erbi infiorate e di selvaggie rose!
e poi lo volli il dì che mi fu detto:
"Ecco la tua livrea!" — e, come fu la sera,
mentre tu studïavi il minuetto,
io, gallonato e muto,
aprivo o rinchiudevo una portiera...
Ah, poscia un'altra sera io l'ho voluto!
Fu quella sera allor che dentro all'anima
mi venne il gran disio di farti mia.
Per te sognavo il genio!... Ma, ironia!
sovra altra fronte già splendea: Chénier!

Ed il destin che trama le commedie
de le diverse vite, quasi a prologo
quella sera ci unìa!... Vidi il tuo amore!
Innamorato e odiando son fuggito!...
e poscia no non m'ha Chénier ferito
ma il grido tuo d'orrore, il tuo: Gérard!...
Pure anche allora, e sempre, t'ho voluta!
La poesia in te cosi gentile,
di me fa invece un pazzo grande e vile!
Ebben? Che importa? Sia!
E, fosse un'ora sola,
io voglio quell'ebbrezza
de' tuoi occhî profondi!
Io pur, io pur, io pur voglio affondare
le mani mie nel mare
de' tuoi capelli biondi!...
Or dimmi che farai contro il mio amore?

MADDALENA.

Là... giù!... nella via corro!... Il nome mio
vi grido!... Ed è la morte che mi salva!

(*Gérard va a frapporsi tra Maddalena e le due uscite*)

GÉRARD.

No, tu non lo farai! — No! tuo malgrado
tu mia sarai!

MADDALENA (*gittando un grido di terrore fugge; ma, presa da improvvisa idea, movendo risoluta verso Gérard gli dice:*)

Se de la vita sua
tu fai prezzo il mio corpo... ebbene, prendimi!

GÉRARD (*da sé*).

Come sa amare!

MADDALENA.

La mamma morta
m'hanno a la porta
là de la stanza mia;—
moriva e mi salvava!...
poscia — a notte alta — io con la Bersi errava,—
quando, ad un tratto, un livido bagliore
guizza e rischiara innanzi a' passi miei
la cupa via!—
Guardo!... Bruciava il loco di mia culla!

MADELEINE (*entering.*)
Can I see Charles Gerard?

MATHIEU.
Here, this way, please!

MADELEINE.
Maybe no longer you remember me?
Who knows! I'm Madeleine de Coigny!
Ah! drive me not away!
Since, if you will not hear me, I am lost!

GÉRARD.
For you was I waiting;
'Tis I that brought you here;
'Tis I that have beset your path
With swarms of crafty spies!
Watching in street and by-way,
Mine eye at ev'ry moment
Was always fixed upon you;
Thus, to secure you, I have seized your lover!

MADELEINE.
Well, here am I! Take your revenge!

GERARD.
Nay, not revenge!

MADELEINE.
Takee your revenge. I am the last survivor of my house.

GERARD.
Nay, not revenge!

MADELEINE.
Then wherefore would you have me here?

GERARD.
Why would I have your here?
Because I desire you!
Because 'tis written thus i' the book of Fate;
Because my will would have it so, my will supreme
'Tis Fate's decree; and lo! 'tis come to pass!
For you I long'd while yet a little maid,
With me you wander'd
A-down the daisied meadows,
Thro' fragrant lane in blossom,
Adorn'd with wilding roses!
For you I long'd that day they told me:
"Here! don thy liv'ry"
And when at evening,
As there you practis'd the measure of a minuet,
I, rigid, mute, in liv'ry,
Threw back or closed the curtains at the doorway.
And now, once more do I desire you!
It is the charm, the poetry of your presence
That doth enrage me, goad me on to madness!
What matter? Be it so!
Tho' 'twere but one short hour,
I'll feast me on the beauty of those eyes enthralling!
I, too, I hunger for your soft caresses—
Would plunge my hand within the ocean
Of those bright golden tresses!
Say, who shall save you now from my great love?

MADELEINE.
I'll rush thro' all the streets,
Denounce myself to the mob!—
From death, say, who shall save me, then?

GÉRARD *barring her passage.*
That you shall never do!
Ah! tho' you hate me, you are mine!

MADELEINE (*shrieks and endeavors to escape; then, suddenly, with great calmnes, she aproaches him.*)
If you will save his life
At the price of my honor—
I am yours! Take me!

GERARD (*aside*)
Ah! how she loves him!

MADELEINE.
Ere death had taken
My darling mother
Leaving me forsaken,
In dying, she strove to save me!
In darkest midnight I fled with Bersi;
The suddenly a lurid glare
Lit up the path that lay before.
The cruel flames my home devour'd,

Così fui sola!... E intorno il nulla!
Fame e miseria!...
Il bisogno e il periglio!...
Caddi malata!...
E Bersi, buona e pura,
(ed a narrarlo mancan le parole)
ha del suo corpo fatto
un mercato, un contratto
per me!—Porto sventura
a chi bene mi vuole!
Fu in quel dolore
che a me venne l'amore!...
Voce gentile piena d'armonia
che mi susurra: "Spera!"
e dice: "Vivi ancora! Io son la vita!
Ne' miei occhi è il tuo cielo!
Tu non sei sola! Le lagrime tue
io le raccolgo!... Io sto sul tuo cammino
e ti sorreggo il fianco
affaticato e stanco!...
Sorridi e spera ancora!... Son l'amore!...
Intorno è sangue e fango?... Io son divino!...
Io sono il paradiso!... Io son l'oblio!...
Io sono il dio
che sovra il mondo scende da l'empireo,
muta gli umani in angioli,
fa della terra il ciel!...
Io son l'amore!
L'angiol tremante allor le labbra smorte
della mia bocca bacia... E or vi bacia la morte!...
Corpo di moribonda è il corpo mio!
Prendilo, dunque!... Io son già morta cosa!...

GÉRARD (*guardando dei fogli che gli vengono consegnati*).
Perduto!
Ah, la mia vita per salvarlo!

MADDALENA.
Voi lo potete!... Appena stamattina
egli arrestato fu.

GÉRARD.
Ma per Chénier
un uomo che l'odiava ha preparato
per oggi il suo giudizio... la sua morte!...
(*A un tratto dalla strada viene un mormorio, un bisbiglio di folla.*)
La folla già!... La maledetta folla
curiosa ed avida di sangue e lacrime.
(*Rumore dei fucili e delle baionette*)
Sono i gendarmi!...
E là sta già Chénier!

MADDALENA (*disperatamente*)
Salvatelo! Salvatelo! Salvatelo!

GÉRARD.
Ah, la Rivoluzione i figli suoi
divora!... Non perdona!... Fin di sangue
per tutti...
(*scrivendo un biglietto al Vice Presidente Dumas.*)
Io l'ho perduto?... Lo difenderò!
Il tuo perdono è la mia forza! Io spero!
(*il pubblico, si rovescia tumultuante, rumoroso, eccitato, nell' aula.*)

CORO DI VECCHIE
Mamma Cadet!...
Presso alla sbarra, qui!
Di qui si vede e si ode
a perfezione.
Qui si gode
la vista d'ogni cosa.
Voi state bene?
Sì.
E voi?
—Così... così...
Dal mercato venite?...
Vengo dalla barriera!...
Notizie ce ne avete?...
No! E voi nulla sapete?...
Hanno cresciuto il pane!...
Eh lo so... è un tiro...
Dite!
È un tiro di quel cane
d'inglese detto Pitt!

UN'ALTRA.
Venite?

L'AMICA.
Sì!

MATHIEU.
Un po' di discrezione,
cittidina!...

CORO DI VECCHIE
Più in là!
Venite qua,
cittadina!...
Dite, oggidì
grande infornata, pare!
Sì.
Molti ex!

(*Entrano giudici e giurati*).

And I was homeless, with nought before me
But hunger, misery, and peril dire!
Then I fell sick, and Bersi nurs'd me,
On me spent all her savings, noble soul!
To such as love me, see, I bring misfortune!
'Twas in such sorrow
That first I heard the voice of Love!
In accents sweet, it murmur'd:
"The Star of Love shall guide thee,
"E'en tho' grief betide thee!
"Love, the immortal fire from heaven,
"Boon to mourners given,
"Love's self am I; oh, hear me calling:
"I'll guard thee, guide thee, save thee from falling!
"Hope on, hope ever!
"Love fails thee never!
"Tho' dark the road, and foes assail thee,
"I will not fail thee;
"I am Love whose magic pow'r,
"My name is Love!
"Like golden sunlight falling from the skies,
"All this world can change to Paradise!
"Love's very self am I!"
And then the angel kiss'd me:
In me that hour the light of life did die!
Take me, then, take me; but a corpse am I!

(*Papers are handed to Gerard.*)

GERARD (*reading*).

He's lost. I'd give my life to save him!

MADELEINE.

Ah! you can save him!
This morning only was he arrested!

GERARD.

But one who hates him
Has hurried on his case for trial;
And he must die!

(*Sounds of the noisy crowd heard without.*)

The cruel mob comes back,
Athirst for blood and tears and carnage!

(*Clatter of soldiers' arms.*)

Do you hear their sabres clanking?
They're the gendarmes; they've got him, in there!

MADELEINE (*despairingly*).

Ah! save him!

GERARD.

Thus doth the Revolution
Devour the sons that serve her!
(*Writing a note for presentation to the President of the Court.*)
Your sweet forgiveness shall make me bold!
Courage! 'tis not too late;
I'll save him, if I can!

(*The mob now noisily enters the Court.*)

CHORUS.

Well, how are you?
I'm just so-so!
Have you come back from market?
No, from the barrier.
You've heard the news? No!
Not heard the news?
They've raised the price of bread!
Yes, yes! I know!
They say 'tis all that scoundrel,
That English villain, Pitt!

ONE OF THEM.

Are you coming?

A FRIEND.

Here I am!

MATHIEU.

Now, then, what a noise you're making!

CHORUS OF OLD WOMEN.

Mother Cadet! sit by the barrier, here!
Here's the best place for seeing and hearing!
Come over here, good Mother Babet!
Here one sees things to perfection.
There'll be lots of prisoners!
There's Legray! And a poet! Come this way!
Move up, do! No, I sha'n't!

(*Enter the Judges and Jury.*)

MATHIEU.
E c'e un poeta!
l'asso ai giurati, o popolo!

GÉRARD (a Maddalena).
Eccoli, i giudici.

LE MERCATINE (si levano ritte sulle panche esaminando i giudici).
Chi presiede é Dumas!...

ALTRI (nominando i giudici.)
Vilate...

MERCATINE.
... pittore!
L'altro è lo stampatore
tribuno Nicolas!...

UNA VOCE.
Ecco laggiù Fouquier!...

TUTTI.
L'accusatore pubblico!...

MADDALENA (a Gérard).
E gli accusati?...

GÉRARD (indicando la porta).
Di là... presso ai giurati!

MADDALENA (vedendo schiudersi la porta, soffocando un grido).
Ecco...

GÉRARD.
Tacete!

MADDALENA.
Mi manca l'anima!
(Entrano i prigionieri)

MADDALENA.
Egli non guarda!... Non mi crede qui!...
Ma pensa a me! Io sono in quel pensiero!...

MATHIEU.
Silenzio!

DUMAS (leggendo i nomi).
Gravier de Vergennes.

FOUQUIER TINVILLE (legendo una nota).
Un ex referendario!
(fa un rapido gesto e ripone la nota)

PUBBLICO.
È un traditore!
(succede un silenzio profondo)

DUMAS (legge un altro nome)...
Laval Montmorency...

FOUQUIER-TINVILLE (c. s.).
Convento di Montmartre!

CALZETTAJE, MERCATINE, PESCIVENDOLE (urlano).
Aristocratica!

IL PUBBLICO (le grida ironico).
A che parlar?... Sei vecchia!... Taci

DUMAS.
Ti tolgo la parola! Abbiamo fretta!
(La monaca lascia cadere uno sguardo di sprezzo—poi siede dignitosa.—Il pubblico la applaude deridendola.)

DUMAS (c. s.)
Legray!
(Si leva una donna giovane che vuol parlare ma é zittita dal pubblico e si lascia cadere sulla panca piangendo.)

DUMAS.
Andrea Chénier!

GÉRARD (a Maddalena).
Coraggio!

MADDALENA (guardando Chénier).
O amore! o amore!

PUBBLICO.
Ecco, è il poeta!
Fouquier Tinville attentamente legge!
Lunga è l'accusa dunque!
È un accusato
pericoloso?
Sì!

MATHIEU.
Scrittore... e basta!

FOUQUIER TINVILLE.
Andrea Chénier, poeta giornalista.
Costui violento scrisse contro agli uomini
de la Rivoluzione. Fu soldato
con Dumouriez e...

PUBBLICO.
Un traditor!

CHÉNIER (a Fouquier Tinville).
Tu menti!

GÉRARD (fra sè, terribile, con disperazione a Maddalena).
Ah, Maddalena, io sono che ciò feci!

DUMAS (a Chénier).
Siediti e taci!

MATHIEU.
Make way for the jury!

GERARD (*to Madeleine*).
Those are the judges.

CHORUS.
Here they come, the judges!
That's the President Dumas!
There's Vilate, the painter!
The other one's a printer, Tribune Nicolas!
See! there he goes! That's Fouquier,
The great Attorney-General!

MADELEINE (*to Gerard*).
Where are the accused?

GERARD (*pointing to door*).
In there, next to the jury!

MADELEINE (*as the door opens*).
Heavens! My courage fails me!

(*The prisoners enter; Chénier walks last.*)

He does not heed us!
Perchance he thinks of me!

MATHIEU.
Silence!

DUMAS (*reading out the names.*)
Gravier de Vergennes—

FOUQUIER-TINVILLE (*consulting his notes.*)
An ex-Chancery officer!

(*Motions the accused to be seated.*)

CHORUS.
Then he's a traitor!

DUMAS (*reading*).
Laval Montmorency—

FOUQUIER-TINVILLE.
From the convent of Mont-Martre!

CHORUS.
A cursed aristocrat!
Best hold your tongue, you hag!
Silence! Die! Ha! ha! ha!

FOUQUIER-TINVILLE.
I can't let you speak; we are in a hurry.

GERARD (*to Madeleine.*)
DUMAS (*reading*).
Legray—
(*A woman rises, and would speak, but is silenced by the mob. She sinks back, sobbing piteously.*)

DUMAS (*reading*).
André Chénier—

Courage!

MADELEINE (*gazing at Chénier*).
Belov'd one!

CHORUS.
There's the poet!
Fouquier-Tinville reads the charge with interest;
No doubt that he's a dang'rous fellow.

MATHIEU.
A writer—that's all!

FOUQUIER-TINVILLE.
He has written against the Revolution;
Was a soldier with Dumouriez—

CHORUS.
He's a traitor!

CHÉNIER (*to Fouquier*).
You lie!

GERARD (*to Madeleine.*)
'Twas I who thus denounc'd him!

DUMAS (*to Chénier.*)
Silence!

Gérard (*fortissimo*).
Parli!

Alcuni.
Parli!

Tutti (*interessandosi*).
Parli!

Dumas (*violento*).
No, nego la parola!

Tutti.
Parli! Parli!

Chénier.
Sì, fui soldato
e gloriosa affrontata
ho la morte che vil qui mi vien data.
Fui letterato,
ho fatto di mia penna arma feroce
contro gli ipocriti!
Colla mia voce
ho cantato la patria!
Pura la vita mia
passa nella mia mente
come una bianca vela;
essa inciela
le antenne, ali allargate
ad un eterno volo,
al sole che le indora,
e affonda
la spumante prora
ne l'azzurro dell'onda...
Va la mia nave spinta dalla sorte
a la scogliera bianca de la morte?...
Son giunto?... E sia!
Ma ancor io salgo a poppa e una bandiera
trionfal disciolgo ai venti!
De' mille e mille miei combattimenti
è la bandiera e su vi è scritto: "Patria!"
(*verso Fouquier Tinville*)
A lei non sale
il tuo fango, o Fouquier!
Essa ognora s' insola
immacolata.
Essa è immortale!
Non sono un traditore.
Uccidi? E sia! Ma lasciami l'onore.

Fouquier Tinville (*subito*).
Udiamo i testimoni!

Gérard (*con voce possente*).
Il passo datemi!
Carlo Gérard.

Dumas.
Sta bene; puoi parlare.

Gérard.
L'atto d'accusa è orribile menzogna.

Fouquier Tinville (*sorpreso*).
Se tu l'hai scritto?!

Gérard.
E ho denunciato il falso
Or lo confesso.
(*un gran movimento*)

Fouquier Tinville.
Io non ti credo!

Gérard.
Giuro!

Dumas.
Dinne il perchè.

Gérard.
L' odiavo!

Dumas.
Non ti credo!

Fouquier Tinville (*levandosi ritto e picchiando febbrilmente sul foglio scritto da Gérard*).
Mie faccio queste accuse e le rinnovo!

Dumas.
Ti do il consiglio di tacerti!

Gérard.
No!
Il tuo consiglio è una viltà!

Fouquier Tinville.
Tu offendi
la patria e la giustizia!

Il Pubblico.
Basta! Taci!
Imponigli silenzio tu, o Dumas!

Mercatine.
In istato d'accusa dichiaratelo!

Sanculotti.
Sì; fuori della legge!

Tutti.
Alla lanterna
Esso è un sospetto!
Fu comprato!
Taci!

GERARD.
Let him speak!

CHORUS.
Speak, then! Prove you're not guilty!

DUMAS.
I will not allow it!

CHORUS.
Let him speak!

CHÉNIER.
Aye, as a soldier
Once I faced a glorious death,
Not such a vile one as you offer!
I was a writer; and I made my pen a
    scourge
Wherewith to lash all lying hypocrites!
And, as a poet, ever sang my coun-
    try's praise.
Life was for me a ship
Set in a boundless ocean
With snowy sail outspread
To catch the morning glory;
It rode upon the crested waves,
Forth to remote horizons.
Now is my bark the sport of Fate,
And driven upon the rocks,
The ghostly rocks of Death.
Will it founder? Maybe!
But lo! from the mast
Floats a bright banner triumphant in
    the breeze;
Thereon is writ, "My Country!"

(*to Fouquier-Tinville.*)

Your filth shall never soil that banner!
In truth am I no traitor!
Kill me, 'tis well! But leave my ho-
    nour bright!

FOUQUIER-TINVILLE.
Now we'll hear the witnesses!

GERARD (*forcing a passage through
the crowd*).

Let me pass! I'm Gerard!

FOUQUIER-TINVILLE.
'Tis well! Speak!

GERARD.
The indictment is a monstrous lie!

FOUQUIER-TINVILLE (*astonished*).
'Twas you who wrote it!

GERARD.
But the charge is a false one, I con-
    fess it!

(*Sensation*).

FOUQUIER-TINVILLE.
I don't believe it.

GERARD.
I swear it is true.

FOUQUIER-TINVILLE.
Why did you do that, then?

GERARD.
I hated him.

DUMAS.
I don't believe it.

FOUQUIER-TINVILLE.
(*Pounding the papers containing the
indictment.*)
I, too, have made these charges,
Now I repeat them!

DUMAS.
I advise you to keep silent.

GERARD.
Then such an act is vile!

FOUQUIER-TINVILLE.
'Tis an insult to country, to justice!
Enough!

THE AUDIENCE.
Let Dumas silence him!

FISHWIVES.
Indict him!

SANCULOTS.
Outlaw him!

ALL.
Ha! most suspicious! They've brib'd
    him!
Silence!

GÉRARD.
La patria? La giustizia osi tu dire?
La tua Giustizia ha nome Tirannia!
L'amore della patria?! Qui?!... No, è un' orgia
d' odî e vendette!... Il sangue della patria
qui còla!... E siam noi stessi che feriamo
il petto della Francia!...
Basti il sangue!
Andrea Chénier della Rivoluzione
è figlio! — È il figlio più glorioso suo!...

MERCATINE e CALZETTAJE.
Con gli accusati tosto giudicatelo!
Alla lanterna!
Morte!
Alla lanterna!

(*lontano rullare i tamburi*)

GÉRARD.
Laggiù, è la patria! Odila, o popolo!
È la sua voce!...
Eccola!... E là la patria;
ove si muore colla spada in pugno!
Non qui dove le uccidi i suoi poeti!
(*Gérard corre a Chénier e lo abbraccia.*)

CHÉNIER.
O generoso! O grande!.. Vedi?... lo piango!

GÉRARD.
Guarda laggiù!... Quel bianco viso... È lei!

CHÉNIER.
Lei?
Maddalena!... Ancor l'ho riveduta!
Or muojo lieto!

GÉRARD.
Io spero ancora!
(*i giurati rientrano.*)

DUMAS.
(*dà una rapida occhiata al verdetto*).
Morte!

FOUQUIER TINVILLE.
Via i condannati!

MADDALENA.
(*mentre Chénier esce*)
Andrea!..
Rivederlo!...

CALA LA TELA

QUADRO QUARTO

(*Il cortile delle prigioni di San Lazzaro a mezzanotte. Andrea Chénier scrive a tavolino Roucher gli è vicino.*)

SCHMIDT (*a Rouchert*).
Cittadino, men duol, ma è tardi assai.

ROUCHER (*dandogli del denaro*).
Pazienta ancora un attimo!...

CHÉNIER. (*cessa di scrivere*).
Non più...

ROUCHER.
Ah, leggi!...

CHÉNIER.
Pochi versi...

ROUCHER.
Leggi! Leggi!

CHÉNIER.
Come un bel dì di maggio
che con bacio di vento—e carezza di raggio
si spegne in firmamento,
col bacio io d'una rima,
carezza di poesia—salgo l'estrema cima
de l'esistenza mia.
La sfera che cammina
per ogni umana sorte—ecco già mi avvicina
all'ora della morte,
e forse pria che l'ultima
mia strofe sia finita,—m'annuncierà il carnefice
la fine della vita.

(*con grande entusiasmo.*)

Sia!—Strofe, ultima Dea,
dà ancor al tuo poeta—la sfolgorante idea,
la fiamma consueta;
io, a te, mentre tu vivida
a me sgorghi dal cuore,—darò per rima il bacio
ultimo di chi muore.

(*Roucher e Chénier si abbracciano e poi si separano.*)

GERARD.

Here, all your justice is but cruel tyranny!
An orgie vile of hate and vengeance!
Can such as you be counted patriots?
Bloodthirsty villains, ye, who stab the heart of France!
Chénier's a son of the glorious Revolution;
Crown him with laurel, never let him die!

(*A sound of drums heard without.*)

Hear ye it, citizens?
There speaks the real Fatherland,
Whose gallant sons all perish for her now!
Not here, where they are murdering her poets!

(*Rushes to Chénier and embraces him.*)

CHÉNIER.

Oh, noble heart and gen'rous! See my tears!
(*Exeunt Jurors*).

GERARD.

Look, over there, yon pallid face! 'Tis she!

CHÉNIER.

She? Madeleine?
I've seen her once again!
Now I die happy!
(*The jury come back into court.*)

GERARD.

I yet have hope!

DUMAS

(*glancing at the verdict handed to him by the foreman*).
Death!

FOUQUIER-TINVILLE.

Lead them away.

MADELEINE

(*as Chénier is lead away*).
André! André! Farewell!

CURTAIN.

ACT IV.

(*The Courtyard of the Prison of S*t*. Lazare at midnight. André Chénier seated at a table, writing. Roucher is beside him.*)

SCHMIDT (*to Roucher*).

I'm sorry, but the hour is late!

ROUCHER (*giving him money*).

Nay, wait a moment longer!

CHÉNIER (*as he stops writing*).

'Tis done!
Verses?

CHÉNIER.

Just a few lines.

ROUCHER.

Read them!

CHÉNIER.

"Like summer day that closes
"While the breezes are sighing
"All for love of the roses,
"In dreamy twilight dying;
"So now my life hath ending,
"As yet one last kiss tender
"The Muse doth now accord me
"Ere I to Death surrender.
"The joys of life are over;
"Fond Hope doth now forsake me;
"Love is lost to the lover;
"Lo! cruel Death must take me.
"As in these lines the Heav'nly Muse
"Farewell to me is calling,
"The headsman grim shall summon me
"To meet my doom appalling!
(*with great enthusiasm.*)
"Hail! Poetry, glorious goddess!
"Unto thy votary, oh! grant, I pray thee,
"The living flame of fancy, the fir sublime, immortal!
"Behold this song I bring to thee,
"Blent with my sighing,
"Let one last strain of melody
"Greet thee from poet, dying!"
(*Roucher and Chénier embrace and then part.*)

(*Si picchia al portone della prigione.
Entrano Gérard, e Maddalena.*)
SCHMIDT (*gli s'inchìna deferente.*)
Tu qui, Gérard?

GÉRARD.
Viene a costei concesso
un ultimo colloquio...

SCHMIDT (*interrompendolo*).
Il condannato?...
Il nome?

MADDALENA.
Andrea Chénier!

SCHMIDT.
Sta ben!
Attendi!

MADDALENA (*a Gérard, risoluta*)
Il vostro giuramento vi sovvengo!
(*rivolgendosi a Schmidt*).
Odi! Fra i condannati di dimani
è una giovane donna.

SCHMIDT.
La legray!

MADDALENA.
Or ene... viver deve!

SCHMIDT.
Cancellare
or come da la lista il nome suo?

MADDALENA.
Che importa il nome se in sua vece
un' altra per lei risponderà?

SCHMIDT.
Sta ben!... Ma, e l'altra?

MADDALENA.
Eccola!

SCHMIDT.
Come?!... Lei?...
Tu, cittadina?

MADDALENA.
(*a Schmidt porgendogli pochi giojelli
e una piccola borsa contenente alcuni luigi*).
A voi!... Giojelli son!... Questo è denaro.

SCHMIDT.
Evento strano in tempo di assegnati!
Io non vorrei...
Capite?... Io non so nulla!...
(*A Maddalena*)
Al nome di Legray... salite in fretta!...
(*esce*)

GÉRARD.
O Maddalena, tu fai della **morte**
la più invidiata sorte!

MADDALENA.
Benedico il destino!
Benedico la morte!

GÉRARD.
Salvarli!... Ancor da Robespierre!...
Ancora!
(*esce*)
(*Schmidt ritorno con Chénier*).

CHÉNIER.
Vicino a te s'aqueta
l'irrequìeta anima mia;
tu sei la mèta
d'ogni desio e bisogno
e d'ogni sogno
e d'ogni poesia!...
⑯ Entro al tuo sguardo
l'iridescenza scerno
de li spazî infiniti, lo son già eterno!
Ti guardo;
e in questo fiotto verde
di tua larga pupilla erro coll'anima!...
Questa è la luce arcana
delle plaghe serene!...
Mi avvolge! Si allontana
lungi e si perde
ogni ricordo di cose terrene!...
Tu sei la poesia
che alfin si dona tutta al suo poeta!
Tu sei la mèta
dell'esistenza mia!
Il nostro è amore d'anime!

MADDALENA.
Il nostro è amore d'anime!

CHÉNIER.
Che tu viva se muojo, di', che vale?
È l'anima immortale;
ovunque tu sarai, sì, io là sarò!

MADDALENA.
⑯ Per non lasciarti
son qui; non è un addio!
Vengo a morire,
vengo a morire anch'io
con te!...
Finì il soffrire....
La morte nell'amarti!...
Chi la parola estrema
dalle labbra raccoglie
è Lui... l'Amor! Come gemine foglie
da l'albero di vita
cadiamo e il vento
ne avvolge insieme dentro alla infinita
luce del firmamento!...

(*Knocking heard without. Enter Gerard and Madeleine*).

SCHMIDT (*bowing respectfully*.)
You here, Gerard?

GERARD.
This lady is permitted to have a final interview with—

SCHMIDT (*interrupting*).
Which prisoner?
Tell me his name.

MADELEINE
André Chénier!

SCHMIDT.
'Tis well! Wait!

MADELEINE (*to Gerard*).
The oath that you have sworn to me remember!

(*to Schmidt.*)

Listen! Among those who are to die to-morrow, there is a young woman!

SCHMIDT.
Yes, Legray!

MADELEINE.
Well, mark you, she must live!

SCHMIDT.
But how from the death-roll can I now strike off her name?

MADELEINE.
The name is nothing, if, when she's called, another should reply!

SCHMIDT.
And who is that other?

MADELEINE.
'Tis I!

SCHMIDT.
You? You would replace her?

MADELEINE (*giving jewels and gold.*)
See, here! I'll give you these! Money and jewels!

SCHMIDT.
'Tis an evil wind that blows no good to some one!

(*to Gerard*).
I hardly like to risk it!
Well there! I know nothing!

(*to Madeleine.*)
But—when I call for Legray, at once come forward!
(*Exit.*)

GERARD.
Oh! Madeleine thy love victorious
Make shameful death most glorious!

MADELEINE.
Blessed Fate that requites us!
Blessed Death that unites us!
GERARD (*aside*).
How to save them? I'll go once more to Robespierre!
(*Exit.*)

(*Schmidt returns with Chénier.*)

CHÉNIER.
From thee, belov'd, my restless soul
New joy and peace doth borrow;
The goal art thou of my desire,
The solace of my sorrow;
In thy blue eyes gazing,
All Heav'n appears before me,
Starry spaces, bright and boundless;
The gates are they, the shining portal
Of a fair realm immortal,
Where I with thee would dwell!

MADELEINE.
Our love is of the soul, divine

CHÉNIER.
'Tis thou that art the life of me

MADELEINE.
With thee I'll stay to the last,
Nor say farewell!
With thee to die have I come!

In quell'ora suprema
de l'ultimo cammino
ogni dolor finisce
col tuo bacio; il divino!...
Ah, se anche è del carnefice
la man che insiem ci unisce,
quella sua mano è pia
se la tua boca—tocca
la morta bocca mia.
Salvo una madre! Maddalena all'alba
ha nome per la morte Idia Legray!
Vedi? La luce incerta del crepuscolo
giù pe'squallidi androni già lumeggia.
Abbracciami, mio amante! Amante,
baciami!

CHÉNIER.
Orgoglio di bellezza!
Trionfo tu de l'anima!
O mia fortuna il premio
di questa tua carezza!
Il tuo amore, sublime amante, è mare,
è ciel, luce di sole e d'astri... È il
mondo!

CHÉNIER.
La nostra morte è il trionfo d'amore!

MADDALENA.
La nostra morte è il trionfo d'amore!

CHÉNIER.
Viva la morte!

MADDALENA.
Viva la morte!

CHÉNIER.
È la morte!

MADDALENA.
È la morte!

CHÉNIER.
Ella viene col sole!

MADDALENA.
Ella vien col mattino!

CHÉNIER.
Benedico la sorte!

MADDALENA
Benedico il destino!

CHÉNIER.
Vien come l'Aurora...

MADDALENA.
Col sole che la indora!

CHÉNIER.
Ne viene a noi dal cielo
velata entro ad un velo...

MADDALENA.
fatto di rose e viole!

CHÉNIER.
Viene la misteriosa!

MADDALENA.
La eterna innammorata!

CHÉNIER.
Viene la Eterna Cosa...

MADDALENA.
La amante immacolata!

CHÉNIER.
La fronte essa mi sfiora
come raggio d'aurora!

MADDALENA.
Ci bacia è ci accarezza
lene si come brezza!

CHÉNIER.
Come una brezza lene
la morte, eccola, viene!

CHÉNIER e MADDALENA.
(*abbracciati l'uno all'altro*).
Nell'ora che si muore
eterni diveniamo!...
Eternamente amiamo!...
Morte è infinito, è amore!...

SCHMIDT, GENDARMI, SECONDINI
(*ripetono forte il nome appellato dal
l'Usciere*).
Andrea Chénier!

CHÉNIER.
Son io!

SCHMIDT, GENDARMI, SECONDINI
Idia Legray!

MADDALENA.
(*si fa arditamente innanzi*).
Son io!

CHÉNIER.
Inni alla morte!

MADDALENA.
Viva la morte!
(*si avviano al patibolo*).

CALA LA TELA.

All suffering ended! By death to thee united!
Let the last word upon my lips be this:
"I love thee!"
When comes the morning,
Madeleine goes to death as Idia Legray!

CHÉNIER.
Pride of beauty.
Triumph of the soul!
Thee, my happy thought,
The prize of my good luck!
Thy love, my queen, is for me
A sea, a heaven, a sun,...
The very light of day,... 'tis all!

CHÉNIER.
Our death is love's triumph!

MADELEINE.
Our death is the crown of love!

CHÉNIER.
I welcome Death!

MADELEINE.
Welcome, welcome!

CHÉNIER.
It is coming!

MADELEINE.
Death is coming!

CHÉNIER.
It is coming with the sun beams!

MADELEINE.
Death comes in the wake of morn

CHÉNIER.
Happy is my lot!

MADELEINE.
Blessed is destimy!

CHÉNIER.
Death comes on the wing of dawn!

MADELEINE.
With the morning golden light!

CHÉNIER.
From heaven to us it comes!
Shrouded in a wondrous veil....

MADELEINE.
Of violets and roses fair.

CHÉNIER.
There it comes, the misterious

MADELEINE.
The ever restful Death!

CHÉNIER.
There comes the everlasting end.

MADELEINE.
The beloved maiden pure!

CHÉNIER.
She, with her lps my forehead smites
Like the morning rays of dawn!

MADELEINE.
Her loving fond embraces
New joy and peace afford.

CHÉNIER.
New joys and peace affords us
Kind Death,... Here it comes!

(*Chénier and Madeleine embrac.*)
The passing of our lives
Is the dawn of our eternal love!
Love be our everlasting bond!
And Death immortal love!

SCHMIDT, GENDARMES AND GUARDS
(*calling the prisoners.*)
André Chénier.

CHÉNIER.
'Tis I!

SCHMIDT, GENDARMES AND GUARDS
Idia Legray!

MADELEINE.
(*boldly coming forward.*)
'Tis I!

CHÉNIER.
Let us to death, united
Raise our song!

MADELEINE
O, blissful Death!

(*They go out to the scaffold*).

CURTAIN.

Printed in Great Britain
by Amazon